Administration of the Marine Mammal Protection Act of 1972

Annual Report

January 1, 1999 to December 31, 1999 and January 1, 2000 to December 31, 2000

U.S. Department of the Interior

U.S. Fish and Wildlife Service
Biological Resources Discipline/
U.S. Geological Survey

MARINE MAMMAL PROTECTION ACT

Report of the Department of the Interior

The Marine Mammal Protection Act of 1972 (16 U.S.C. 1361-1407, 86 Stat. 1027 (1972)), as amended (95 Stat. 979 (1981), 98 Stat. 440 (1984), 100 Stat. 3741 (1986), 102 Stat. 4755 (1988), and 108 Stat. 532 (1994)), states in Section 103(f) that:

> "Within six months after the effective date of this Act [December 21, 1972] and every twelve months thereafter, the Secretary shall report to the public through publication in the Federal Register and to the Congress on the current status of all marine mammal species and population stocks subject to the provisions of the Act. His report shall describe those actions taken and those measures believed necessary, including where appropriate, the issuance of permits pursuant to this title to assure the well-being of such marine mammals."

The responsibility of the Department of the Interior is limited by Section 3(12)(A)(ii) of the Marine Mammal Protection Act to those marine mammals that are members of the Orders Carnivora (polar bear, sea otter, and marine otter), Pinnipedia (walrus), and Sirenia (manatees and dugong). Accordingly, published herewith is the report of the Department of the Interior for the periods of January 1, 1999, to December 31, 1999, and January 1, 2000, to December 31, 2000, on the administration of the Marine Mammal Protection Act with regard to those mammals.

Issued at Washington, D.C.

DIRECTOR
U.S. Fish and Wildlife Service

7/29/04
Date

ASSOCIATE DIRECTOR FOR BIOLOGY
Biological Resources Discipline
U.S. Geological Survey

8/15/04
Date

Administration of the Marine Mammal Protection Act of 1972

Annual Report

January 1, 1999 to December 31, 1999 and January 1, 2000 to December 31, 2000

Administration of the Marine Mammal Protection Act of 1972

Annual Report

January 1, 1999 to December 31, 1999 and January 1, 2000 to December 31, 2000

U.S. Department of the Interior
U.S. Fish and Wildlife Service
U.S. Geological Survey/Biological Resources Division
Washington, D.C. 20240

Table of Contents

List of Acronyms

1973 Agreement - 1973 International Agreement on the Conservation of Polar Bears

ABSC - Alaska Biological Science Center, USGS

Act - Marine Mammal Protection Act of 1972

ADFG - Alaska Department of Fish and Game

ANC - Alaska Nanuuq Commission

ASOC - Alaska Sea Otter Commission

BBNA - Briston Bay Native Association

BPXA - BP Exploration (Alaska), Inc.

CDFG - California Department of Fish and Game

CFR - Code of Federal Regulations

CITES - Convention on International Trade in Endangered Species of Wild Fauna and Flora

Corps - United States Army Corps of Engineers

CSC - California Science Center

Department - Department of the Interior

DNA - Deoxyribonucleic acid

ESA - Endangered Species Act of 1973, as amended

EVOS - Exxon Valdez Oil Spill

EWC - Eskimo Walrus Commission

FCSC - Florida Caribbean Science Center, USGS

FDEP - Florida Department of Environmental Protection

FDNR - Florida Department of Natural Resources

FFWCC - Florida Fish and Wildlife Conservation Commission

FLIR - forward-looking infrared imagery

FMP - Florida Marine Patrol

FMRI - Florida Marine Research Institute

FY - Fiscal Year(s)

GDNR - Georgia Department of Natural Resources

GIS - Geographic Information System

HCH - hexachlorocyclohexane

IGC - Inuvialuit Game Council

IPCoMM - Indigenous Peoples Council on Marine Mammals

K - carrying capacity

LOA - Letter of Authorization

MIPS - Manatee Individual Photoidentification System

MMC - Marine Mammal Commission

MML - Mote Marine Laboratory

mtDNA - mitochondrial Deoxyribonucleic acid

MTRP - Marking, Tagging, and Reporting Program

NAVSTA ROOS RDS - United States Naval Station, Roosevelt Roads, Puerto Rico

NMFS - National Marine Fisheries Service

NMML - National Marine Mammal Laboratory

NSB - North Slope Borough

NVPP - Nearshore Vertebrate Predator Project

NWHC - National Wildlife Health Center

NWR - National Wildlife Refuge

PBR - potential biological removal

PCB - polychlorinated biphenyls

PIT - passive integrated transponder

ppm - parts per million

PRDNR - Puerto Rico Department of Natural Resources

PTT - platform transmitter terminals

QA/QC - quality assurance/quality control

SAR - stock assessment report

Service - United States Fish and Wildlife Service

SFWMD - South Florida Water Management District

SNI - San Nicolas Island

TASSC - The Alaska Sea Otter and Steller Sea Lion Commission

TDRs - time-depth recorders

TTINWR - Ten Thousand Islands National Wildlife Refuge

UHF - ultra-high frequency

UMMH - Chukotka Union of Marine Mammal Hunters

USCG - United States Coast Guard

USGS/BRD - United States Geological Survey, Biological Resources Discipline

VHF - very-high frequency

WERC - Western Ecological Research Center, USGS

WHMP - Walrus Harvest Monitoring Project

Introduction

The passage of the Marine Mammal Protection Act of 1972, hereafter referred to as the Act or MMPA, gave the Department of the Interior (Department) responsibility for manatees, polar bears, walruses, sea and marine otters, and dugong. Within the Department, the U.S. Fish and Wildlife Service (Service) is the primary agency responsible for managing these marine mammals and for enforcing the moratorium on taking and importing marine mammals and marine mammal parts. During 1999 and 2000, the Biological Resources Discipline (formerly the Biological Resources Division) of the U.S. Geological Survey (USGS/BRD) was responsible for conducting marine mammal research.

The Service administers requests for waiving the moratorium and for the transfer of management authority to States, issues permits, enforces provisions of the Act, and publishes rules and regulations to manage marine mammals. The Service also cooperates with the States, and participates in international activities and agreements. In addition, the Service lists and delists species as endangered or threatened and undertakes other Endangered Species Act (ESA) related responsibilities and maintains a close working relationship with the Marine Mammal Commission (MMC) and its Committee of Scientific Advisors. Prior to Fiscal Year 1994, the Service conducted the marine mammal research program.

Presently, the USGS/BRD has been charged with that responsibility; the Service closely coordinates with the USGS/BRD on marine mammal research needs.

During the two-year period of time covered by this report, there were no significant changes to the listed status of any of the species of marine mammals whose management is the Service's responsibility.

SPECIES LIST

Species List and Status of Marine Mammals Under Service Jurisdiction Under the Act and the ESA

Species		Marine Mammal	Endangered
Common Name	Scientific Name	Protection Act	Species Act
Polar bear	Ursus maritimus	Yes	No
Sea otter-Alaska	Enhydra lutris kenyoni	Yes	No
Sea otter-southern	Enhydra lutris nereis	Yes	Threatened
Marine otter	Lutra felina	Yes	Endangered
Walrus	Odobenus rosmarus	Yes	No
Dugong	Dugong dugon	Yes	Endangered*
West Indian manatee	Trichechus manatus	Yes	Endangered
Amazonian manatee	Trichechus inunguis	Yes	Endangered
West African manatee	Trichechus senegalensis	Yes	Threatened

* The dugong is listed as endangered throughout its entire historic range except when it occurs in the United States.

1

Summary of the Program for 1999 and 2000
Appropriations

The Act's funding authorization for the Department occurs in Section 116(b). Spending occurs on a Fiscal Year (FY) basis. Calendar years 1999 and 2000 covered by this report overlap FYs 1999, 2000, and 2001. Funds (in $000) authorized for these years, as well as funds spent in FY 1999 and FY 2000, and projected to be spent in FY 2001, are presented.

	Authorized	*Expended*	*Projected*
Fiscal Year 1999	$10,296	$3,633	--
Fiscal Year 2000	$10,296	4,701	--
Fiscal Year 2000	$10,296	--	$5,000

	Actual FY 99	Actual FY 00	Actual FY 01
Marine Mammal Protection Act Expenditures			
USGS/BRD Research and Development			
Alaska sea otter	$ 325	$ 742	$ 749
Polar bear	335	414	533
Pacific walrus	50	80	250
Misc. marine mammals (including polar bear, walrus, and sea otter)	100	112	120
Total USGS/BRD Research and Development	$ 810	$1,348	$1,652
Management			
Permit activities	$ 195	$ 200	$ 205
Law enforcement activities	620	800	790
Other management activities	2,008	2,353	2,353
Total Management	$2,823	$3,353	$3,348
MMPA Grand Total	$3,633	$4,701	$5,000
Endangered Species Act Expenditures			
Section 6 (Grants-to-States)			
California - sea otter	$ 0	$ 0	$ 0
Florida - manatee	0	0	0
Georgia - manatee	26	26	26
Total Section 6	$ 26	$ 26	$ 26
Section 15 (USGS/BRD Research and Development)			
Endangered/threatened otters	$ 233	$ 290	$ 691
Manatee	456	533	347
Total USGS/BRD Research and Development	$ 810	$ 823	$1,038
Section 15 (Management)			
Consultation[1]	$ 320	$ 320	$ 320
Recovery[1]	352[2]	551[3]	1,025[4]
Hawaiian monk seal[5]	75	75	75
Total Management	$ 747	$ 946	$1,420
ESA Grand Total	$1,462	$1,795	$2,484

[1] *Funded under authority of the ESA. Includes funds for all endangered and threatended marine mammals for which the Service engages in consultation and recovery activities.*

[2] *In Fiscal Year 1999, $152,000 in special project funds is included in the "Manatee" total above in Section 15 (USGS/BRD Research and Development) and is not included here.*

[3] *In Fiscal Year 2000, funds shown include a $498,000 add-on for manatee protection zone enforcement and $53,000 for manatee special projects, whicle $62,500 in special project funds are included in the "Manatee" total above in Section 15 (USGS/BRD Research and Development) are not included here.*

[4] *In Fiscal Year 2001, funds shown include a $1,000,000 add-on for manatee protection zone enforcement and $25,000 for manatee special projects, while $98,000 in special project funds are included in the "Manatee" total above in Section 15 (USGS/BRD Research and Development) and are not included here.*

[5] *Although the National Marine Fisheries Service (NMFS) has primary responsibility for Hawaiian monk seals according to Section 3(12)(A)(i) of the Act, almost the entire world population of the seals breeds and forages in the Hawaiian islands, Midway Atoll, and Johnston Atoll National Wildlife Refuges. Funds reported are spent for monk seal activities on Refuge lands under aithority of the National Wildlife Refuge System Administration Act of 1966 (16 U.S.C. 668dd-668ee).*

Outer Continental Shelf Operations and Environmental Studies

No activities were reported for either year covered by this report.

Research and Development

Part of DOI's responsibility in implementing the MMPA is to monitor the health of marine mammal populations and to manage them in a way that ensures they are maintained at their optimum sustainable population. In order to accomplish this, we conduct studies to help us understand the potential impacts to marine mammals of both natural events and anthropogenic activities. Information obtained in these studies enables us to work with individuals and industries that are operating in areas occupied by marine mammals and to develop and implement effective management strategies. For example, the oil and gas industry in Alaska has regularly requested that we promulgate regulations under Section 101(a)(5)(A) to authorize the incidental, unintentional taking of polar bears and Pacific walrus in the course of industry activities. Incidental take regulations provide an opportunity for DOI to interact with industry to minimize potential effects on marine mammals. We conduct studies to support the regulations, which can only be promulgated if the Secretary finds that the incidental taking has no more that a negligible impact on the species. Findings from these studies provide a basis for improved future impact assessment and mitigation. These studies, many of which are specifically requested and supported by industry, are described below.

The USGS/BRD conducted research under the Act during FYs 1999 and 2000 at several Centers and Field Stations. The Alaska Biological Science Center (ABSC) is responsible for polar bear, walrus, and northern (i.e., Alaska) sea otter research. The Western Ecological Research Center (WERC), formerly the California Science Center (CSC), is responsible for work on southern sea otters. The Florida Caribbean Science Center (FCSC) is responsible for research on sirenians (manatees and dugongs). The Division of Cooperative Research administers additional research at cooperative units across the country funded by, and in support of, the needs of the Service, other USGS/BRD Research Centers, and other bureaus of the Department.

For each project active during FY 1999 and 2000, the project title and summary, followed by highlights of accomplishments are given below by species. Previous results and accomplishments can be found in earlier publications.

1. Polar bear

A. Project Title and Summary:

Mapping of high probability maternal denning habitats of polar bears.

Polar bears give birth in dens of ice and snow to protect their highly altricial young. Disruption of the denning cycle may result in mortality of their young. In northern Alaska, terrestrial dens occur within the Prudhoe Bay oilfield and in other regions of the arctic coastal plain under consideration for petroleum exploration and extraction. Most exploration and construction occurs during the winter months when maternal dens are occupied. Temporal and spatial management of human activities is necessary to avoid negative consequences that may result from disturbing maternal dens. While the chronology of maternal dens is understood, habitat considerations are not well known.

1999 and 2000 Activities/ Accomplishments

Many new polar bear dens have been discovered in northern Alaska since this project began in 1995. During 1999, data were collected and used for digital map adjustments and error checking. Final ground truthing was completed in 1999. Maps, documentation, and publications were prepared during the year.

During 2000, we visited 25 den sites, located previously by radiotelemetry, to characterize physiognomy of known denning locations.

High-resolution aerial photographs (n=3000) were then searched for the kinds of habitats recorded at actual dens. We used characteristics of the observed dens and aerial photos to identify 1782 km of bank habitats suitable for denning. Bank habitats comprised 0.18 percent of our study area between the Colville River and the Tamyariak River in northern Alaska. A final digital map, which identified 82 percent of bluff denning habitat in this region, and the documentation of how the map was developed will be published in the journal ARCTIC. This product will help minimize potential for disruptions of maternal dens by winter petroleum exploration activities.

In the summer of 2001, we continued to accrue data related to polar bear den characteristics by visiting those additional dens and incorporating their characteristics into our database. As human activities in the Arctic expand, these new data will help us update and revise information on the distribution of probable den habitat.

FY 1999	$30,000
FY 2000	$0
FY 2001	$20,000

Polar bear cubs

B. Project Title and Summary:

Population ecology of polar bears in western Alaska and adjacent portions of Russia.

Polar bears are seasonal residents of the Bering and Chukchi Seas during ice bound months of November through May. However, knowledge of seasonal use patterns and densities of polar bears in the Bering and Chukchi Seas was largely unknown. Polar bears were captured throughout the Bering and Chukchi Seas adjacent to the Alaskan and Russian coastlines in the spring and adult females were fitted with satellite telemetry collars that provided regular position locations using overflying satellite technology. Data from these satellite instrumented polar bears indicate that the Chukchi Sea population is shared with Russia. These data are being used to delineate the population bounds and define the seasonal limits of polar bear distributions in the Bering and Chukchi Seas.

This effort will also determine the degree of discreteness between the adjacent populations. Detailed movement data currently available is limited to adult females as male polar bears cannot be fitted with neck collars. A pilot study of subcutaneous implantation of satellite transmitters with percutaneous antennae was conducted to determine the feasibility of using this technology to test the assumption that adult male polar bears have similar movement patterns as adult females.

Polar bears have long life spans, delayed maturity, small litter sizes, and extended reproductive intervals. These population characteristics indicate that any increases in direct mortality of polar bears may not be compensated by increased productivity of polar bears. We are in the process of building new simulation models that will help understand the degree to which industrial activities and other anthropogenic influences may alter polar bear survival and recruitment patterns.

1999 and 2000 Activities/ Accomplishments

During the 2-year period, we finished a new analysis of mark and recapture data collected from polar bears over a 30+ year period.

This analysis provided us with the best yet estimates of population size and trend of polar bears in Alaska.

Knowledge of population size and trend is necessary to manage anthropogenic risks to polar bears. Despite capturing over 1,025 females between 1967 and 1998, previously calculated estimates of the size of the southern Beaufort Sea population have been unreliable. We improved estimates of numbers of polar bears by modeling heterogeneity in capture probability with covariates. Important covariates referred to the year of the study, age of the bear, capture-effort, and geographic location.

Our best model suggested an increase from around 500 females early in the study to as many as 1,500 at the end of the study. Assuming the increase in numbers of males was comparable to that recorded for females, this could suggest a total population size of over 2,500 animals, many more than previously hypothesized. The mean coefficient of variation on estimates for the last decade of the study was 0.16, the smallest yet derived.

Despite the significant improvements in estimates provided by this new estimator, we recommend a conservative approach to management of polar bears in the southern Beaufort Sea. The estimated growth rate of the population of 1.035 is near the maximum that seems possible for a hunted polar bear population and should be viewed cautiously. Likewise, simulation studies suggested there might be a small positive bias in when the data set contains significant heterogeneity. Cautious harvest management, therefore, still is advised. Collection of a more intensive southern Beaufort Sea mark-recapture data set is necessary in order to further refine our population estimates.

FY 1999	$150,000
FY 2000	$319,000
FY 2001	$300,000

C. Program Title and Summary:

Detection of denning polar bears with forward-looking infrared (FLIR) imagery.

Polar bears construct maternal dens of ice and snow throughout their circumpolar range. In the Beaufort Sea region of northern Alaska, most dens have been found on the flat coastal plain. Hydrocarbon extraction is now occurring or planned along 100 miles of the Beaufort Sea coastline. If development occurs in the National Petroleum Reserve in the future, the scope of development could include up to 2/3 of the northern coastal region of Alaska. These human activities can disturb polar bears and are a potential threat to denning polar bears.

While numbers of humans and their activities have increased in northern Alaska, numbers of denning females present along the coast also have increased. Satellite-monitored platform transmitter terminals (PTTs) will transmit daily through the predenning and denning period. Transmissions will convey location, temperature, and activity level of the bear, allowing us to ascertain the timing and location of den entry. The effectiveness of FLIR to detect denned bears will be tested December-February, by which time dens will be well established and covered by a thick snow layer. A series of overflights will be recorded on videotape for each den located. Overflights will differ in altitude, speed, view angle, and ambient conditions. A panel of observers, then, will test visibility of bears in dens, and we will record whether they successfully see the dens. After den abandonment in spring, we will return to each den to record habitat features that could influence detectability of the den by FLIR.

1999 and 2000 Activities/ Accomplishments

In both years, final testing of the ability of FLIR to detect polar bears in their dens was hampered by poor weather. We hypothesized that clear and cold weather early in the winter when the snow pack is thin should be ideal for detection of the heat signature of a den. Unfortunately, these weather conditions were not available during the winter of either year.

During the winter of 1999-2000, we knew the locations of seven maternal polar bears dens. Snow, sleet, fog, and even rain were the predominant weather conditions we faced while testing the ability of FLIR to detect dens under the snow. Moisture in the air is one condition that we know prohibits transmission of infrared radiation, and hence, it was not surprising that we detected only 3 of 7 known dens.

The winter of 2000-2001 carried forth with the same kinds of weather observed the previous year. We had concluded from previous testing that FLIR flights should be conducted early in the winter, when snow depths are lower. Also, in early winter the sun is always below the horizon, preventing solar warming from adding competing hot targets to the otherwise cold landscape. Unfortunately, during 3 weeks of standby with a Bell 212 helicopter, the weather was neither good enough to fly, nor good enough to test FLIR.

However, in January, although we still had low clouds and fog on most days, conditions generally were better, and there were a few days during which we actually had clear, if not cold, air. Of 12 dens visited, we were able to detect seven. We believe we may have detected one other den; however, due to solar warming, there were many warm targets in the vicinity of the radio-collared bear, and we cannot be sure that we assumed correctly the heat signature to be the heat signature of the den.

Final analyses of data collected is scheduled to be performed at a future workshop, and recommendations for use of the FLIR system will be made in a final report prepared thereafter. But, even without detailed analyses three conclusions are obvious: (1) FLIR surveys must be performed as early as possible in winter to minimize snow depths over the dens; (2) clear and preferably cold air conditions will always provide superior viewing conditions with FLIR; (3) and even a small amount of solar exposure compromises the detectability of dens with FLIR.

FY 1999	$100,000
FY 2000	$95,000
FY 2001	$160,000

D. Project Title and Summary:
Oil spill/polar bear interaction modeling.

The polar bear is the apical predator of the arctic, and may be among the most important indicators of general ecosystem health. Polar bears are most common near the continental shelf, an area also rich in extractable hydrocarbons. The goal of this project is to estimate the number of polar bears that might be oiled by a hypothetical spill from the Liberty Oil Production Island and sub-sea-floor pipeline in the central Beaufort Sea.

1999 and 2000 Activities/ Accomplishments

The relative probability distribution of polar bears in Alaskan near-shore and offshore waters will be presented in a report summarizing the distribution and its ramifications. Probability distributions will be depicted as grid cell densities and as a 2-dimensional surface overlaying the arctic ocean with contours of polar bear distribution. That surface will be in the form of an ARC/Info GIS coverage. An article for the refereed journal Arctic was prepared describing the method and results.

Because we are interested in the relative probability of seeing any polar bear, not just a radio-collared bear, we need an accurate estimate of the sampling fraction. Sampling fraction, the proportion of the population observed (by radio telemetry) during the study, is calculated as the number of observed animals divided by the population size. Hence, accurate population estimates are needed to calculate relative probability distributions. Therefore, a second product from this project was an article submitted to the Canadian Journal of Zoology describing the estimation procedure we used to determine population size. In addition, the projection model was prepared (as well as a manual for its use), and an article describing its development and results was submitted to Arctic.

In 2000, we used 10,913 reobservations of 289 satellite radio-collared females to estimate the distribution of polar bears in the Beaufort Sea. We used 255 observations of 69 polar bears and 322 observations of 95 polar bears to estimate the distribution of polar bears in the Liberty study area in September and October, respectively. We assumed that other members of the population moved similarly to females.

Oil spill footprints for October and September, the times during which we hypothesized effects of an oil-spill would be worst, were estimated using real wind and current data from 1980-1996. We used ARC/Info software to calculate overlap (numbers of bears oiled) between oil-spill footprints and polar bear grid-cell values. Numbers of bears potentially oiled by a 5,912 barrel spill ranged from 0 to 25 polar bears for open water conditions, and from 0 to 61 polar bears in autumnal mixed ice. Oil-spill trajectories affected small numbers of bears far more often than they affected larger numbers of bears. Median numbers of bears oiled by the 5,912 barrel spill in September and October were 1 and 3 bears, respectively.

FY 1999	$55,000
FY 2000	$0
FY 2001	$53,000

2. Alaska sea otter

A. Project Title and Summary:
Processes structuring coastal marine communities in Alaska.

Surveys of relative abundance and distribution in Glacier Bay and Icy Straits are in progress. Field work on a study of sea otter foraging behavior is underway and data management is in progress. Annual field reports to Glacier Bay Park on sea otter distribution and food habits are available. Field work was initiated in 1996 on sea otter diving behavior using ultra-sonic transmitters and time-depth recorders. Data from diving studies are under management, manipulation, and analysis.

1999 and 2000 Activities/ Accomplishments

Since 1995, the number of sea otters in Glacier Bay has increased from 5 to more than 500 animals. Most of this growth resulted from immigration of individuals outside the Park. Sea otter distribution is limited to a few locations, all in the lower portions of Glacier Bay, and large areas throughout the Bay do not contain persistent sea otter populations.

In 1999, 14 of 21 time depth recorders deployed were recovered. Also in 1999, studies began of the species composition, abundance, and size class distribution of intertidal clams and urchins in Glacier Bay and Icy Straits.

In 2000 studies on the species composition, density, and size class distributions of intertidal clam populations in and near Glacier Bay were completed. A total of 85 intertidal sites were sampled, including 12 sites where sea otters have been present for about 20 years, 14 sites where otters have been present for about 10 years, and 59 sites where otters are either absent or in the process of re-colonizing.

We found mean clam densities in lower Glacier Bay of about 95/m2, and about 10/m2 in the two upper arms. Where sea otters have been present for one and two decades, clam densities were about 10/m2 and 30/m2, respectively. Patterns in estimates of clam biomass generally followed density patterns, although clam species preferred by sea otters (Saxidomus and Protothaca) were generally larger in Glacier Bay compared to where sea otters have been present for more than 20 years.

Sea otters are now well established in limited areas of the lower portions of Glacier Bay. It is likely that distribution and numbers of sea otters will continue to increase in Glacier Bay in the near future. Sea otter diet consists primarily of clams, mussels, urchins, and crabs, but varies on relatively small spatial scales. Glacier Bay supports large and diverse populations of intertidal clams that presently are largely unexploited by sea otters. It is predictable that the density and sizes of intertidal clam populations will decline in response to otter predation. This will result in fewer opportunities for human harvest, and will also result in ecosystem level changes, as prey are modified for other predators, such as octopus, sea stars, fishes, birds, and mammals.

Sea otters will also modify benthic habitats through excavation of sediments required to extract burrowing fauna, such as clams. Effects of sediment disturbance by foraging sea otters are not understood. Glacier Bay also supports large populations of other preferred sea otter prey, such as king and Dungeness crabs, green sea urchins, and several clam species that are commercially, culturally, or ecologically important. As the recolonization of the Bay by sea otters continues, it is also likely that dramatic changes will occur in the species composition, abundance, and size class composition of many components of the near-shore marine ecosystem. Many of the changes will occur as a direct result of predation by sea otters. Other changes will result from indirect or cascading effects of sea otter foraging, such as increasing kelp production and modified prey availability for other near-shore predators.

FY 2000 $210,000
FY 2001 $180,000

B. Project Title and Summary:
Assessment of sea otter population status in Alaska.

With the exception of 13 small remnant populations, sea otters were extirpated from their historic range in the north Pacific Ocean during the 18th and 19th centuries. Since the beginning of the 20th century, through protection and reintroduction, sea otter populations have increased in abundance and distribution such that most of their range in Alaska, with the exception of southeast Alaska, is currently occupied. Although data are incomplete, there is evidence of increasing, stable, and declining sea otter populations in different areas of the Pacific.

The cause, magnitude, and geographic extent of the declining populations are unknown. Additionally, harvest levels of sea otters for subsistence have increased over the past 10 years. Population level effect of the harvest at current levels are unknown. Because sea otter populations occur over vast and remote areas, determining population status and trends through traditional survey methods is logistically difficult and fiscally expensive. Two active study plans describe the research under this program. One research project includes estimating sea otter activity time budgets (i.e., the proportion of time an individual or population allocates to foraging, resting, or other behaviors). The method employed consists of deploying time-depth recorders (TDRs) on individual otters. These devices record and store depths at 2 second intervals. The second

Sea otter

David Menke/USFWS

active study plan involves monitoring environmental contaminants in the nearshore marine ecosystem in the central and western Aleutian Islands.

1999 and 2000 Activities/ Accomplishments

Work continued on methods to assess sea otter population status, and on the collection and archival of biological specimens acquired in cooperation with the Service and the Alaska Sea Otter Commission (ASOC), now the Alaska Sea Otter and Steller Sea Lion Commission) to be used in population assessment studies. In 1999 work continued on estimating activity time budgets from time depth recorders (TDR's) in southeast Alaska. We were successful in recovering 14 of 21 instruments deployed in 1999 and data analysis of the 16 TDR's recovered to date is under way. In 2000 we initiated a cooperative program with the Monterey Bay Aquarium to apply the TDR technology to the threatened California sea otter population.

Following is a brief, preliminary summary of the TDR results. Theoretically, the proportion of time an individual spends foraging is inversely related to food availability, thus providing a measure of population status relative to food resources. For the 13 animals thus far analyzed, we have identified a total of 230,209 dives of three different types: zero-bottom time, traveling, and foraging. Each dive type has different attributes such as depth, duration, bottom time, and rate of ascent and descent. Mean dive depth of >105,000 foraging dives were 19.6 m (se=3.5) and mean maximum dive depth was 60.5 m (se=6.3) among the 13 individuals. The minimum maximum dive depth for an individual was 35.5 m and the maximum dive depth for an individual was 100 m. On average,

male sea otters made fewer dives than females (5,004 males vs > 10,719 for females), but dove deeper, on average, than females (33.6 m males vs 12.0 m for females). In terms of activity time budgets, both male and female sea otters spent about 55 percent of their time resting and 12 percent traveling. However, male sea otters spent only 24 percent of their time foraging, compared to 31 percent for females. Male sea otters spent 8 percent of their time in other activities (zero-bottom time dives) compared to only 2 percent for females.

In 2000, work was completed on applying molecular genetics (mtDNA) to discriminate sea otter populations throughout the species range. Work on evaluation of the effects of population bottlenecks on sea otter genetics was completed. Work was also completed on a project to distinguish levels of population structuring within the Alaska subspecies of sea otters.

We also completed work in 2000 on life history plasticity and population regulation in sea otters. We contrasted body condition, and age-specific reproduction and mortality between a growing population of sea otters at Kodiak Island and a high-density, near-equilibrium population at Amchitka Island, Alaska. Sixty-two percent of the preweaning pup losses at Amchitka occurred within a month of parturition and 79 percent occurred within two months. Postweaning survival was also low at Amchitka as only 18 percent of instrumented pups were known to be alive one year after mother-pup separation. Adult survival rates appeared similar at Amchitka and Kodiak. Factors affecting survival early in life thus are a primary demographic mechanisms of population regulation in sea otters. By maintaining uniformly high reproductive rates over time and limiting investment in any particular reproductive event, sea otters can take advantage of unpredictable environmental changes favorable to pup survival. This strategy is consistent with predictions of "bet-hedging" life history models.

Publication completed 12/25/1999: Scribner, K.M., J.L. Bodkin, B.E. Ballachey, S.R. Fain, M.A. Cronin and M. Sanchez. 1997. Population genetic studies of the sea otter (Enhydra lutris): A review & interpretation of available data. Proceedings: Marine Mammal Genetics Symposium, La Jolla, CA. Sept., 1994.

Publication completed 4/1/1998: Bodkin, J.L., B.E. Ballachey, M.A. Cronin & K.T. Scribner. 1999. Population demographics and genetic diversity in sea remnant and translocated sea otter populations. Conservation Biology 13(6) 1378-1385.

Presentation completed 12/4/1999: Monson, Daniel, H., J. Watt, T. Gelatt, J.L. Bodkin, J.A. Estes and D.B. Siniff. 1999. Estimating foraging time budgets for sea otters from characteristics of foraging behavior. 13th Beinnial Marine Mammal Conference, Maui, Hawaii. 29 Nov.-3 Dec. 1999.

Presentation completed 12/1/1999: Bodkin, James L., K.A. Kloecker and A.M. Burdin. 1999. Fluctuating asymmetry and genetic diversity in sea otters. 13th Beinnial Marine Mammal Conference, Maui, Hawaii. 29 Nov.-3 Dec. 1999.

Publication completed 10/1/1999: Bodkin, J. L. and M.S. Udevitz. 1999. An aerial survey method to estimate sea otter abundance. in: Garner, G.W., S.C. Amstrup, J.L. Laake, B.F.J. Manly, L.L. McDonald, and D.G. Robertson, (eds.) Marine mammal survey and assessment methods. Balkema Press, Netherlands pg. 13-26.

Publication completed 2/2/2000: Gorbics, C and J.L. Bodkin. Stock Identity of sea otters in Alaska. in press. Marine Mammal Science.

Presentation completed 1/18/2000: Lowry, L., D. DeMaster and J.L. Bodkin. 2000. Status of marine mammals populations in the Gulf of Alaska. 11th annual Exxon Valdez oil spill symposium 18-19 January 2000, Anchorage, AK.

Dissertation completed 6/1/2000: Fukuyama, A.K. 2000. The ecology of bivalve communities in Prince William Sound, Alaska: Influence of the Exxon Valdez oil spill and predation by sea otters. Doctoral dissertation, University of Washington, Seattle.

Publication completed 10/1/2000: Monson, D.H., D.F. Doak, B.E. Ballachey, A. Johnson, and J.L. Bodkin. 2000. Long-term impacts of the Exxon Valdez oil spill on sea otters, assessed through age-dependent mortality patterns. Proceedings National Academy of Sciences, USA.97(12):6562-6567.

FY 1999	$60,000
FY 2000	$90,000
FY 2001	$120,000

C. Project Title and Summary:
Patterns and processes of population change in selected nearshore vertebrate predators.

The purpose of this study is to track the recovery process of sea otters (Enhydra lutris) in western Prince William Sound through annual aerial surveys of abundance and to monitor the abundance and size distribution of a preferred sea otter prey, the green sea urchin (Stronglycentrotus droebachiensis). Study History: This project began in April 1999 with the approval of a 5-year plan by the Exxon Valdez Oil Spill (EVOS) Trustee Council. The project is an extension of Restoration Project 93043-2, designed to develop an aerial survey method for sea otters in 1993, and the Nearshore Vertebrate Predator Project (NVPP), 95025 (SIS 5001228) designed to assess recovery of the nearshore ecosystem affected by the Exxon Valdez oil spill.

This project supports an annual survey of sea otter abundance in Prince William Sound, population estimates from intensive surveys in an oiled and unoiled area and estimates of the density and sizes of green sea urchins from those same intensive study areas.

Sea otters and harlequin ducks occupy an invertebrate-consuming trophic level in the nearshore and are conspicuous components of the nearshore ecosystem. In 1995, the NVPP was initiated to examine the status of recovery of nearshore vertebrates (including sea otters, harlequin ducks, river otters, and pigeon guillemots), and to evaluate possible causes for the apparent lack of recovery. Results of the NVPP clearly suggest that complete recovery has not occurred for sea otters and harlequin ducks.

This proposed work follows up on the critical elements revealed by the NVPP studies, in particular the relation between population status and oil contamination, and evaluation of population status. In addition to observations made directly on predator species, as part of the NVPP, we have

observed an apparent response among several invertebrates to reduced sea otter densities. This finding represents a shift in the ecological processes structuring the nearshore community and provides a unique opportunity to test predictions related to sea otter recovery and their prey. We also have an opportunity to test the application of this novel approach as a tool for monitoring predators through prey that may have broader ecological applications.

1999 and 2000 Activities/ Accomplishments

The otter population estimates for Western Prince William Sound were 2,475 (se=381) in 1999 and 2,852 (se=440) in 1998. A single survey of Western Prince William Sound and a series of replicate aerial surveys were completed at Knight and Montague Islands in July 2000. Surveys of sea urchin populations at Knight and Montague Island were completed in August 2000. In July 2000, we estimated the Western Prince William Sound sea otter population at 2,992 individuals (se=480). We estimated population sizes of 79 (se=6) at Northern Knight Island and 544 (se=95) at Montague Island in 2000.

The significant increases we have detected since 1993 in and around the spill area continue to indicate progress toward recovery of the EVOS injured sea otter population. However, the lack of a concurrent increase around Northern Knight Island through 2000, where sea otter mortality was highest, indicate that recovery may not be occurring where oil spill effects were greatest.

Presentation completed 12/1/1999: Bodkin, James L., K.A. Kloecker and A.M. Burdin. 1999.

FY 1999	$95,000
FY 2000	$95,000
FY 2001	$95,000

D. Project Title and Summary:
Interactions between sea otters and nearshore communities.

The sea otter provides one of the best known examples of a keystone species. This study has the following goals: (1) to determine the relative importance of sea otter predation in kelp forest ecosystems across the northeast Pacific Ocean; (2) to understand the breadth of indirect effects of sea otter predation in coastal ecosystems; and (3) to document the effects of environmental contaminants on sea otters, their prey, and other elements of the coastal ecosystems in which they live and interact.

This project began in 1977 when biennial surveys began of translocated northern sea otters to Washington State. In 1989, surveys started being conducted annually and with the cooperation of the Washington Department of Fish and Wildlife. The objective is to monitor the abundance and distribution of the Washington sea otter population to provide data, which will allow a better assessment of population status, and to provide information on growth rates of this population for comparison with populations in California and Alaska.

Studies related to investigating contaminants in mussels and fish include monitoring sea otter populations and kelp forest communities in this Aleutian Islands effort. The rationale for this focus are: (1) sea otters are a known keystone species in kelp forest ecosystems and have high public visibility; (2) otter populations have recently undergone a dramatic decline.

Sea otters compete with humans for shellfish resources. These interactions and conflicts are compounded by the facts that shellfish stocks have declined for reasons other than sea otter predation and coastal marine ecosystems are subject to a wide range of human influences, in particular eutrophication and contamination.

The data will also provide comparative baseline information, which will be extremely valuable in the event of an environmental catastrophe, such as a major oil spill in which a high level of mortality can be expected.

1999 and 2000 Activities/ Accomplishments

Contaminant analyses have been completed on fauna collected. Sea otters have been monitored surrounding Adak Island and other sites.

The findings from this research will be used for the following purposes: (1) to provide a model system for wildlife managers and conservation biologists illustrating the interactions between species and ecosystems; (2) to help the Service develop a working definition for optimum sustainable population; and (3) to assist various management agencies in determining the source, distribution, and effects of environmental contaminants in coastal marine ecosystems of western North America.

By using the fragmented distribution of sea otter populations that resulted from over-hunting during the Pacific maritime fur trade and subsequent protection of the species in the early 1900's as a natural experiment, we have been able to show that sea otters have a wide range of important effects on coastal ecosystems. These include enhancement of primary production, increased competition among kelp species, enhancement of coastal fish populations, and population or behavioral effects on a variety of other consumer species, including gulls, sea ducks, and sea stars. We have also provided evidence suggesting that sea otter predation has shaped the evolution of marine plant/herbivore interactions in North Pacific kelp forests.

Results obtained during the past two years have documented the collapse of kelp forest ecosystems following the reduction of sea otter populations by killer whale predation in western Alaska. Our recent findings also suggest localized contaminant inputs from sites of historic or current military activity in western Alaska, although the evidence suggests that these inputs are not responsible for the population declines. Superimposed on these localized effects is growing evidence for contaminant inputs to western Alaska from Asia, mainly in the form of DDT and its various metabolites. While still not conclusive, there is some recent evidence that these materials may be transported into western Alaska via migratory seabirds. DDE levels in bald eagles that specialize on seabird prey in this region are sufficiently high to cause reproductive suppression.

FY 1999	$170,000
FY 2000	$347,000
FY 2001	$354,000

3. Pacific walrus

A. Project Title and Summary:
Population trends of Pacific walrus.

Pacific walruses occur throughout the Chukchi and Bering Seas and are important to Native subsistence in Alaska and Russia where thousands of animals are harvested each year. Reliable abundance estimates for walrus are currently unavailable. Estimates of the potential biological removal (PBR) level for all marine mammal species are required under a 1994 amendment to the Act. PBR level estimates require an estimate of population size with estimable precision. The status of the walrus population is poorly known, but there are indications that the population

is currently declining from its most recent peak in abundance in the 1980s. Estimates of walrus population trends are critical for effective management.

This study evaluates trends in the walrus population through the establishment of new surveys, evaluation of past data collected from monitoring programs in the U.S. and Russia, and genetic studies to investigate potential structuring in the walrus population.

1999 and 2000 Activities/ Accomplishments

Research planning and project development was conducted. Field work to develop capture and attachment protocols for Pacific walrus were conducted at Cape Peirce on Togiak National Wildlife Refuge. Several types of satellite transmitters were attached to tusks and at-sea locations were obtained. Satellite telemetry data from walrus captured at Cape Peirce indicate a feeding concentration area southwest of the Cape. Russian remotely-sensed ice data are being collected and formatted by Russian cooperators. Ice images of the Bering and Chukchi Seas were processed.

A workshop was held in Anchorage March 27 and 28, 2000, to discuss potential approaches for conducting an aerial survey of the Bering and Chukchi Seas for walrus. Proceedings were published in a Service technical report. An analysis is scheduled to begin in FY 2001 of past haulout count data collected by the Service from mid 1980 to the present from Bristol Bay.

Publication completed: Proceedings of a workshop concerning walrus survey methods, Anchorage, Alaska, March 27-28, 2000. USFWS Technical Report MMM00-2. 92 pp.

FY 1999	$5,000
FY 2000	$20,000
FY 2001	$115,000

Pacific walrus

B. Project Title and Summary:
Pacific walrus telemetry studies.

The distribution of walruses is influenced strongly by the seasonal distribution of pack ice. Herds of mixed sex and age classes occur at sea ice haulouts in winter, primarily in the Anadyr Gulf, St. Lawrence Island, and Bristol Bay regions of the Bering Sea where breeding and calving occurs. In spring, female and young walruses migrate northward with the retreat of sea ice to summer in the Chukchi Sea. Adult males summer primarily in the Bering Sea, using land haulouts on the coasts of Russia and Alaska.

Although these general patterns are known, many aspects of their distribution and movements are poorly understood including their annual fidelity to summering and wintering areas in the Bering and Chukchi Seas, migration routes, and within-season fidelity to local haulouts sites. These studies investigate the seasonal migration patterns, haulout use, and foraging behavior of walruses.

This information will be used to identify potentially separate segments of the population for management purposes and to aid in designing population and behavioral studies.

1999 and 2000 Activities/ Accomplishments

Results from time-depth-recorder data are in press with Marine Mammal Science. Data were collected from four adult animals in 1997 from Bristol Bay and were used to identify dive behaviors and activity of these animals. Analysis of walrus movement data from satellite transmitters deployed over the past five years are underway and are expected to be complete by the end of FY 2001. Plans are being developed to deploy 12 satellite-transmitters in Russian waters in the Gulf of Anadyr in July 2001 to investigate the movement patters of walruses from the hypothesized "Kresta" group.

Publication in progress as of 2/7/2000: Haulout fidelity and feeding areas of male walruses in Bristol Bay, Alaska.

Publication completed 4/13/2001: Jay, C.V., S.D. Farley, and G.W. Garner. in press. Summer diving behavior of male Pacific walrus in Bristol Bay, Alaska. Marine Mammal Science 17:000-000.

Publication in progress as of 4/13/2001; Jay, C.V., and G.W. Garner. submitted. Frequency of location acquisitions from a GPS-Argos satellite unit deployed on Pacific walruses (Odobenus rosmarus divergens). Marine Mammal Science.

FY 1999	$40,000
FY 2000	$60,000
FY 2001	$135,000

C. Project Title and Summary:
Heavy metal contaminants in Pacific walrus.

Anthropogenic pollutants such as heavy metals are commonly found in Arctic marine mammals. Subsistence hunting of these animals may compromise the health of users. The Pacific walrus is a major Arctic subsistence species with thousands harvested annually throughout the Chukchi and Bering Seas. Despite heavy dependence upon walrus for subsistence, very little published information exists concerning potential health risks from ingesting walrus. In addition to their significance to Native subsistence, walrus are ideal sentinel animals for monitoring anthropogenic contamination in Arctic ecosystems. They are apical benthic predators specializing on bivalves, thus their tissue heavy metal concentrations are direct measures of benthic heavy metal loading throughout the Chukchi and Bering Seas. Because of age and sex specific spatial segregation of the walrus population for much of the year, tissues from male walrus harvested in Bristol Bay represent time-integrated sampling of their residence in the Bering Sea, whereas tissues from female and young walrus represent exposures during their summer residence in the Chukchi Sea and winter residence in the Bering Sea.

This project will use walrus tissue samples archived to: (1) make a comparison between two analytical lab techniques in the measurement of metal levels in walrus tissues (National Institute of Standards and Technology traceable standards will be used as the quality assurance/quality control (QA/QC) benchmarks for all laboratory procedures), and (2) provide a data set of metal levels in walrus tissues which will represent information gathered only from samples collected and analyzed under strict QA/QC guidelines.

1999 and 2000 Activities/ Accomplishments

Samples will be acquired from the Alaska Marine Mammal Tissue Archival Project (AMMTAP) and analyzed at the USGS Geologic Division laboratory in Denver, Colorado. Analysis has been delayed due to unforseen delays in tissue acquisition from AMMTAP.

Planned publications from this effort include: (1) Heavy metal contaminants in Pacific walruses, and (2) A comparison of two analytical techniques for determinations of specific heavy metals

and other elements in marine mammal tissues.

FY 1999	$0
FY 2000	$0

D. Project Title and Summary:
Use of stable isotopes and heavy metals in studies of Pacific walrus movements and dietary habits.

Walrus foraging and nutritional ecology are poorly understood. Continued development of Arctic resources, including offshore gas and oil leasing, and the influence of human activities on the Arctic ecosystem have underscored the need to increase our understanding of Arctic biology in order to provide scientifically defensible recommendations to resource managers. The measurement of naturally occurring stable isotopes of C, N, S, O, and H has emerged as an invaluable tool for the investigation of individual and community ecology, as well as ecosystem function.

More recently, stable isotope research in ecology has expanded to include studies of nutritional pathways and the tracking of migratory wildlife. Researchers can obtain a variety of time-integrated diet estimates from tissues because tissue-specific metabolic rates and biochemical pathways cause them to accumulate isotopes at different rates. Tissues such as vibrissae or hair are unique because any segment of these will have an isotopic ratio representative of the consumer's diet just at the time that particular segment was formed. Thus, serial sections from these tissues provide a continuous picture of consumer diet over time, and if the tissue's growth rate is known, diet may be related to seasonal events in the animal's life. Similarly, measures of heavy metal concentrations along the axis of growth in hard tissues such as teeth can provide a history of environmental or dietary exposure of animals to metals such as Hg, Pb, Cu, Zn, Sr, and Ca.

Furthermore, if isotopic and metal profiles are known for geographic regions of the animal's environment, measures of these profiles in tissues can provide information on the animal's residency within geographic areas. The purpose of this work is to explore the use of stable isotope techniques and measures of heavy metals as a tool for studying large-scale movements and dietary habits of walrus.

The stable isotope ratios of N and C will be measured in vibrissae and blood samples of free-ranging male walrus in Bristol Bay and of females and their calves in the northern Bering Sea.

About 30 tooth samples provided by the Service were sectioned and analyzed by Geological Survey of Canada for levels of heavy metal isotopes. These preliminary analyses indicate geographic segregation among male and female animals and between collection sites (harvest villages) within sexes. This suggests that a study based on a larger sample collected over the entire Pacific walrus range may provide information on walrus group affiliation and the distribution of potentially segregated segments of the population.

FY 1999	$5,000
FY 2000	$500
FY 2001	$0

4. Miscellaneous marine mammals

A. Project Title and Summary:
Alaska Marine Mammal Tissue Archival Project.

The cryogenic archival of environmental specimens for retrospective analysis can be an important resource in environmental monitoring programs and for both present and future research on population genetics, pathology, systematics, animal health, and toxicology. The AMMTAP is a joint project conducted by three U.S. Government agencies to collect and archive tissues from Alaska marine mammals. The project emphasizes the use of standardized sampling and archival protocols, procedures that minimize contamination of samples during collection, and maintaining a detailed record of sample history. Most of the animals sampled are from Alaska Native subsistence harvests; therefore, the project requires cooperation and collaboration with numerous Alaska Native organizations and local governmental agencies. Through AMMTAP, samples are collected for contaminant monitoring in the Marine Mammal Health and Stranding Response Program established by TITLE IV of the Act.

In addition, the project has provided samples and/or data for many research programs, both inside and outside the United States, on a variety of subjects. These subjects include genetics research, the circumpolar distribution of chlorinated hydrocarbons in beluga whales, baseline levels of trace elements in tissues, the identification of arsenic and mercury species in marine mammal tissues, biomarker research, nutritional studies, and studies on potential human health effects of Alaska Native subsistence foods.

Presentation completed 1/21/1999: Geoff York. 1999. Alaska Marine Mammal Tissue Archival Project. Focus on the Future-Alaska Environmental Studies, Seventh Alaska OCS Region, Minerals Management Service Information Transfer Meeting. Anchorage, AK

During 2000, AMMTAP samples were obtained and archived from ringed seal, bearded seal, harbour seal, sea otter, polar bear, and bowhead whale. Analysis of ringed seal and polar bear tissues from the Barrow area were also completed resulting in the submission of a publication this spring.

FY 1999	$100,000
FY 2000	$112,000
FY 2001	$120,000

5. Manatee and dugong

A. Project Title and Summary:
Reproduction traits and population dynamics of Florida manatees based on photoidentification techniques.

Long-lived Florida manatees overwinter at natural and man-made warm water sites throughout Florida and in southeastern Georgia. Manatee aggregations reach hundreds of individuals at some of these sites, affording non-intrusive opportunities to record life history observations and photographically document numerous individuals. Photographs and accompanying observational histories also are taken opportunistically at sites frequented by manatees during the non-winter months, and year-round in the course of radio tracking research. Documentation of individual manatees through photoidentification, maintenance of the existing long-term database (20+ years), and determination of survival rates and other population parameters from the database are all highest priority actions in the implementation of the Florida Manatee Recovery Plan. Detailed knowledge of Florida manatee life history and population dynamics is necessary to develop adequate population models.

We continued documentation of individual manatees through photoidentification, maintenance of the long-term database (20+ years), and further development of the Manatee Individual Photoidentification System (MIPS), all high priority actions in the implementation of the Florida Manatee

Recovery Plan. The database currently includes specific identity and feature description data, photographic images, and over 22,000 sighting records and reproductive histories for nearly 1,500 individual manatees.

The data have been converted and are now queried through an Access Database, which currently consists of 26 related tables. The MIPS program and structure has been shared with the Florida Fish and Wildlife Conservation Commission, Florida Marine Research Institute (FMRI), and the Mote Marine Laboratory to assist in maintaining the database on manatees frequenting the southwest coast of Florida. We are also planning to examine the reproductive histories of individual manatees, if differences in age of first reproduction have fitness consequences, and if there are regional differences in fitness.

FY 1999	$124,000
FY 2000	$124,000
FY 2001	$124,300

B. Project Title and Summary:
Use of strip-transect aerial surveys to assess manatee population trends.

The Florida manatee is a large, herbivorous marine mammal that inhabits the coastal waters, estuaries, and freshwater rivers of the southeastern United States, primarily in Florida. Rapid development and increasing human activity in the coastal zone threatens the long-term existence of this endangered species. The Sirenia Project initiated a long-term radiotelemetry study of manatees along the Atlantic coast of Florida and Georgia in 1986 to gather information on the species' ecology, behavior, and life history.

The study has documented individual variation in seasonal movement patterns, migratory behavior in relation to water temperature, areas of high manatee use that vary seasonally, strong site fidelity to warm-season ranges across years, and diel movement patterns. Manatee surveys have typically not been designed to sample quantified survey areas, or to produce estimates of abundance. In 2000, we collaborated with the Service, by designing and analyzing results from strip-transect aerial surveys of the Ten Thousand Islands National Wildlife Refuge (TTINWR). Our objective is to determine if manatee density and distribution in the nearshore waters of the TTINWR and the Everglades

National Park change in response to restoration of natural hydrologic patterns in southwestern Florida. We want to statistically compare pre- and post-restoration indices of manatee abundance using strip-transect surveys in the TTINWR. We established 30 parallel transects, 1 km apart, with a survey strip width of approximately 250 m. The estimates of number of manatees in the study area ranged from 39 to 164, or 0.28 to 1.16 per km5. The estimates for survey dates with conditions ranked as good to very good were 86 to 164. We recommend that at least 6-8 surveys be conducted within a 2-month period, with good to excellent survey conditions to minimize variation among surveys. Surveys should be repeated every year for a minimum of 4-5 years.

FY 1999	$80,000
FY 2000	$80,000
FY 2001	$80,000

C. Project Title and Summary:
Movement, spatial use patterns, and habitat utilization of radiotagged West Indian manatees along the Atlantic coast of Florida and Georgia. Information on movement patterns and habitat requirements of Florida manatees are needed by managers responsible for protecting and recovering this endangered marine mammal. The Sirenia Project initiated a long-term radiotelemetry study of manatees along the Atlantic coast of Florida and Georgia in 1986 and the field work has been completed. The principal goals of this Research Work Order are: (1) to describe within-season movements and spatial use patterns of radiotagged manatees, including home range, core activity areas, travel rates and diel movement patterns; (2) to analyze manatee habitat utilization and preference in two geographic areas of importance to manatees along Florida's east coast; (3) to examine the effects of season, geographic area, age class, sex, and female reproductive status on movement parameters and habitat use; and (4) to determine the accuracy of locations generated from satellite-monitored radio tags, based on field experiments.

1999 Activities/Accomplishments

A total of 83 manatees have been tracked over this ten-year period using conventional field-monitored VHF radiotransmitters and Argos satellite-monitored PTTs, resulting in over 60,000 locations between the Florida Keys and southeast Georgia. A preliminary analysis of manatee winter use of thermal refugia along the Atlantic coast was carried out in the third quarter of 1999 for presentation at a workshop on

manatees and the future of industrial warm-water sources.

FY 1999	$60,000
FY 2000	$60,000

D. Project Title and Summary:
Manatee response to elimination of a thermal refuge north of the species' natural winter range.

Man-made warm water discharges from industries such as power, paper, and chemical-producing plants have enabled manatees to extend their winter range much further north than would be expected for these endangered marine mammals. The natural northern limit of the manatee's range in Florida is thought to be the Sebastian River on the Atlantic Coast, and the Crystal River on the Gulf Coast. Manatees use man-made sources of warm water, as well as natural, warm water springs, to maintain their body temperature during the fall and winter, when ambient water temperatures decline.

An interagency research team is studying the Florida manatee's response to the loss of a significant warm water discharge in northeastern Florida. The Jefferson Smurfit Corp., a paper-products manufacturer in Fernandina Beach, Florida, recently modified its discharge system on the Amelia River. As a result, heated water will no longer be available to manatees in this region, as it has been in past winters. The new system complies with water quality standards regulated by the Florida Department of Environmental Protection (FDEP). Elimination of artificial warm water sources north of the manatee's natural winter range is generally viewed by resource managers as a positive action. Manatees that stay in colder regions because of the availability of industrial effluents are exposed to greater risk of hypothermia during cold winter periods. It is also possible that chronic exposure to cold affects manatee metabolism, reproductive success, and general health. The results of this study will assist resource managers in evaluating the consequences of eliminating specific warm water effluents.

1999 Activities/Accomplishments

Eight manatees were captured and fitted with satellite-monitored radio transmitter assemblies in March 1997, at either the Jefferson Smurfit Corporation effluent basin, or the Georgia Pacific pulp plant in Brunswick, Georgia. Two additional manatees, which had originally been radio tagged at Jefferson-Smurfit in 1996, were retagged without capture, one in February 1997

and one in June 1997. Only one radio tagged manatee has stayed in Brevard County, using the thermal effluents of two power plants in the upper Indian River. Although the sample size is small and the study is still ongoing, it is clear that manatees have a strong affinity for traditional warm water refuges and do not necessarily respond to the absence of a former refuge by returning to more distant sites further south, where warmer water is assured. Some manatees may have been born in the study region and may not have developed the typical manatee migratory pattern. Ongoing development of population genetics techniques may help to resolve this question. It is also clear that secondary warm water sites are more numerous than was previously known, and should not be underestimated in attempts to evaluate the impact of thermal effluent elimination.

FY 1999	$30,000
FY 2000	$65,000

E. Project Title and Summary:
Characterizing benthic habitat and manatee grazing activity in Puerto Rico.

Our objective is to assess the long-term ecological status of seagrass resources in important manatee feeding areas. Unlike the Florida manatee, which utilizes primarily estuarine and freshwater habitats and feeds on a wide variety of submerged, floating, and emergent plants, Antillean manatees in Puerto Rico are found in marine habitats and depend upon seagrasses for food.

The study utilizes radio tracking to reveal manatee movements and habitat use patterns in eastern Puerto Rico, and links them to detailed maps of benthic habitat near the U.S. Naval Station Roosevelt Roads and Vieques Island.

1999 and 2000 Activities/ Accomplishments

Field personnel monitoring the newly tagged individuals have been trained in VHF tracking techniques. Habitat maps for U.S. Naval Station, Roosevelt Roads (NAVSTA ROOS RDS), Puerto Rico, and draft maps for Vieques Island have been produced. Final reports for the mapping effort are in preparation. Copies will be provided to the Navy, Puerto Rico Department of Natural Resources (PRDNR), and other interested cooperators. Annual reports to the PRDNR and the U.S. Navy describe the field methods, databases, and preliminary results on movements and spatial use patterns. The study has documented individual variation in movement patterns and areas of high manatee use. Six study sites, four at Roosevelt Roads Naval Station and two on the west coast of Puerto Rico, near Guanajibo, were assessed in April and December 2000 to determine seagrass distribution, abundance, standing crop, and leaf productivity in manatee feeding areas.

Publication completed: Lefebvre, L.W., J.P. Reid, W.J. Kenworthy, and J.A. Powell. 2000. Characterizing manatee habitat use and seagrass grazing in Florida and Puerto Rico: implications for conservation and management. Pacific Conservation Biology 5(4):289-298.

FY 1999	$35,200
FY 2000	$35,200
FY 2001	$35,200

F. Project Title and Summary:
Postrelease monitoring of captive-reared manatees.

The primary objective of the manatee reintroduction program is to develop protocols and guidelines for releasing long-term captive manatees (captive born and captive reared) into their natural environment. The Sirenia Project represents USGS/BRD in the Interagency/Oceanaria Manatee Working Group (I/O Group), which advises the Service on issues related to captive manatees. The I/O Group recommended the use of a prerelease enclosure as a means of conditioning long-term captives before releasing them in the wild. The Sirenia Project assisted FWS in designing the enclosure; by developing protocols to record observations of manatees; and to assess changes in the aquatic vegetation within the enclosure, radio tracking manatees released from the enclosure, and assisting with postrelease captures and biomedical assessments of reintroduced manatees.

Additionally, the Sirenia Project conducted concurrent satellite transmitter accuracy tests while radio tagged manatees were held in the enclosure. Since 1995, a number of manatee releases have been done directly, in south Florida at Everglades National Park and Biscayne Bay, without prerelease conditioning. Prior to release, each manatee is fitted with a floating, tethered radio tag that is attached to a belt harness around the peduncle. The satellite-monitored PTTs also incorporate a VHF and sonic transmitter to permit tracking in the field. PTT locations are provided by Service Argos, which operates a data collection and location system.

Since April 1993, 17 captive reared and captive born manatees have been released with satellite-monitored radio tags at eight different locations in Florida. The study has documented individual variation in survivability through winters, seasonal movement patterns, areas of high manatee use, strong site fidelity to warm-season ranges across years , and diel movement patterns. Data on blood chemistry, hematology, and body condition have been collected both prerelease and postrelease for most of the manatees studied.

1999 and 2000 Activities/ Accomplishments

Four captive-reared and one rehabilitated manatee were released in the spring run last winter and radio tracked during 2000. The manatees were fitted with satellite-monitored, floating tag assemblies and belt-mounted VHF radio transmitters. Three manatees had gained weight since their release and one was approximately the same weight. All were determined to be healthy, with blubber indices within the range of healthy wild manatees.

Publication completed: Deutsch, C.J. 2000. Winter movements and use of warm-water refugia by radio tagged West Indian manatees along the Atlantic Coast of the United States. Final Report prepared for Florida Power and Light Company and U.S. Geological Survey. 74pp. + append.

Publication completed: Deutsch, C.J., J.P. Reid, R.K. Bonde, D.E. Easton, H.I. Kochman, and T.J. O'Shea. 2000. Seasonal movements, migratory behavior, and site fidelity of West Indian manatees along the Atlantic Coast of the United States as determined by radiotelemetry. Final Report. Research Work Order 163. Florida Cooperative Fish and Wildlife Research Unit, U.S. Geological Survey and University of Florida. 254pp. + xii.

Publication completed: Carr, T. and R.K. Bonde. 2000. Tucuxi (Sotalia fluviatilis) occurs in Nicaragua, 800 km north of its previously known range. Marine Mammal Science 16(2):447-452.

Publication completed: Eros, C., R.K. Bonde, T.J. O'Shea, C. Beck, H. Marsh, C. Recchia, and K. Dobbs. 2000. Procedures for the Salvage and Necropsy of the Dugong (Dugong dugon). GBRMPA Technical Report, Great Barrier Reef Marine Park Authority. Research Publication No. 64. 74 pp.

FY 1999	$65,000
FY 2000	$65,000
FY 2110	$64,600

G. Project Title and Summary:
Manatee population genetics.

The West Indian manatee includes two recognized subspecies, the Florida and the Antillean manatee. The Florida manatee is believed to occur almost exclusively in Florida and neighboring states in the southeastern United States. The Antillean manatee is much more widely distributed, in the Greater Antilles, Mexico, the Caribbean coasts of Central and South America, and the Atlantic coast of Brazil to the state of Bahía. Intensive research efforts over the last 30 years have illuminated aspects of manatee ecology, ethology, and population dynamics.

Research on manatee genetics is mandated by the Service's Florida Manatee Recovery Plan. Such information could improve understanding of the structure and social interactions of populations and thereby influence management objectives for different groups of manatees. Ongoing habitat loss and high mortality rates are factors which threaten the future of the Florida manatee. Low intrinsic reproductive rate and low natural population density make this species particularly vulnerable to human perturbations. One consequence of population reduction is loss of genetic diversity. It is generally recognized that genetic variability is necessary for both adaptation to changing environments and long-term survival of the species. Strategies to preserve genetic diversity require knowledge of the distribution of variation in the populations and species. Several generations of severe inbreeding in a small population or repeated crashes to a few individuals can deplete most of the genetic variation from an initially larger population.

1999 and 2000 Activities/ Accomplishments

A 403 base-pair fragment was examined in 87 individuals from Florida, Puerto Rico, the Dominican Republic, Mexico, Colombia, Venezuela, Guyana, and Brazil, and fifteen haplotypes were identified. Three distinctive mtDNA lineages were observed in T. manatus, corresponding approximately to Florida and the West Indies, the Caribbean coast and rivers of South America, and the Atlantic coast and rivers of South America. The three T. manatus lineages may represent relatively old biogeographic partitions, based on the manatees strong affinity for extensive freshwater habitats in South America, and periodic extinctions of the Florida manatee at the northern end of the species' range during the Pleistocene.

Angela Garcia completed her dissertation, "Genetic Studies of the West Indian Manatee," in April 2000. Eight polymorphic DNA microsatellite loci were identified for use in population analysis. Tissue samples from 223 manatees were analyzed, approximately 45 from each of 5 regions of Florida.

There is significant genetic differentiation between manatees on the east and west coasts; however, no significant differentiation was detected between groups within coasts. The low level of alleles detected for the 8 loci (23 total) indicates a possible bottleneck or founder effect, followed by breeding among related individuals. The Florida manatee population can be considered a single evolutionary unit, which consists of two well-defined management units on the east and west coasts.

Dissertation completed in 2000: Garcia-Rodriguez, A.I. 2000. Genetic studies of the West Indian manatee (Trichechus manatus). Ph.D. thesis. University of Florida, Gainesville, FL. 115 pp.

FY 1999	$15,000
FY 2000	$15,000
FY 2001	$43,000

H. Project Title and Summary:
Evaluation of releases of captive-born and captive-reared manatees.

The primary objective of the manatee reintroduction program is to develop protocols and guidelines for releasing long-term captive manatees (captive-born and captive-reared) into their natural environment. The Sirenia Project represents USGS/BRD in the Interagency/Oceanaria Manatee Working Group (I/O Group), which advises the Service on issues related to captive manatees. The I/O Group recommended the use of a prerelease enclosure as a means of conditioning long-term captives before releasing them in the wild. The Sirenia Project assisted the Service in designing the enclosure, and by developing protocols to record observations of manatees and to assess changes in the aquatic vegetation within the enclosure, radio tracking manatees released from the enclosure, and assisting with postrelease captures and biomedical assessments of reintroduced manatees.

Additionally, the Sirenia Project conducted concurrent satellite transmitter accuracy tests while radiotagged manatees were held in the enclosure. Since 1995, a number of manatee releases have been done directly, without prerelease conditioning, in south Florida (Everglades National Park and Biscayne Bay). Prior to

release, each manatee is fitted with a floating, tethered radio tag that is attached to a belt harness around the peduncle. The satellite-monitored PTTs also incorporate a VHF and sonic transmitter to permit tracking in the field. PTT locations are provided by Service Argos, which operates a data collection and location system. Visual observations of manatee activity, particularly feeding and socializing, provide information on the individual's transition to natural habitats.

1999 and 2000 Activities/ Accomplishments

The 1996 Florida Manatee Recovery Plan mandates the development of protocols and guidelines for captive manatee reintroduction, and for evaluation of reintroduction success. This study provides information critical to the development of sound protocols. Data on manatee survival, movement patterns, food habits, loss of human-friendly behavior, habitat requirements, blood chemistry, and fat metabolism will allow development of protocols and guidelines that can be used by Federal and State managers and veterinarians to establish policies for future manatee releases.

These guidelines and protocols will also be generally useful to periodically assess the condition of wild manatees in other studies, e.g., before and after habitat changes have been imposed.

Manatees rooting in sand

Jim P. Reid/USFWS

I. Project Title and Summary:
Determination and quantification of the diet of Florida manatees in high-use habitats.

The Florida manatee is a herbivorous marine mammal that feeds on a wide variety of marine and freshwater plantsand algae. Manatees occupy a wide variety of estuarine and freshwater habitats in Florida and Georgia.

Determination of the manatee diet is a primary responsibility under the Florida Manatee Recovery Plan. Analysis of diet can supplement field observations that help to identify important areas of habitat requiring protection and the relative importance and extent to which manatees utilize available resources.

The objectives of this research project are: (1) to identify and quantify the relative amount of plant material (seagrasses, algae, freshwater aquatics) by species, and rhizome content, consumed by manatees, through analyses of stomach content samples from salvaged carcasses; and (2) to determine if dietary differences exist among sexes, size classes (relative age), seasons, or specific locations with a general estuarine or freshwater habitat. Techniques for quantifying diet from gastrointestinal tract contents were developed for terrestrial food plants. A hybrid technique was developed for manatee dietary analysis that incorporated components of a microhistological technique and a microscope point technique. This hybrid technique and a protocol for ingesta identification will be utilized in this study, along with a catalog of photomicrographs and a diagnostic key to histological features discernable in masticated material.

1999 and 2000 Activities/ Accomplishments

Information on habitat requirements of Florida manatees is needed by Federal and State managers responsible for protecting and recovering this endangered marine mammal. The Florida Manatee Recovery Plan (USFWS 1996) identifies food habits studies as necessary for full recovery of the species. Data obtained will be available to all clients to assist with manatee habitat assessment and utilization. The procedures and results also may be useful to researchers involved in diet studies of manatees in other parts of their range.

Some of the laboratory work for this ongoing study has been completed. Analyses have been completed on 40 stomach samples from Lee County, 104 from Brevard County, 25 from northeastern Florida and Georgia, and 8 from Puerto Rico. In addition, 50 samples from southwest Florida have been preliminarily analyzed. Hundreds of additional samples from salvaged carcasses are available and will be prioritized for analysis by site and interest from clients. Fecal samples collected from radio tagged manatees are examined on a regular, ongoing basis to assess the food habits of specific, known individuals.

FY 1999 $17,000
FY 2000 $17,000

J. Project Title and Summary:
Seagrass ecology in selected manatee feeding areas

The West Indian manatee is one of few species that graze on living seagrasses, which are an important part of the Florida manatee's diet. Manatees and seagrass have undoubtedly coevolved. We must understand the relationship between seagrass ecology and manatee behavior in order to assure the survival of both resources, which have been and continue to be adversely impacted by humans.

Critically important feeding sites must be characterized to assure that manatee carrying capacity does not decline as a result of changes in manatee population size or distribution, human impacts, or natural phenomena such as sea level rise. Seasonal fluctuations in seagrass species, biomass, leaf rhizome ratio, and nutrients may have important consequences for the nutritional status and life history of the manatee, as has been suggested for dugongs and sea turtles.

1999 Activities/Accomplishments

The results of this research, which concluded in 1999, will help biologists to assess impacts and estimate manatee carrying capacity of repeatedly grazed seagrass beds in areas of special significance to manatee conservation. It will also help to document and elucidate the role of manatee grazing in maintaining seagrass species diversity. Increased awareness of the importance of seagrasses to the future survival of the manatee should also increase public appreciation of the greatly underestimated value of seagrasses in marine and estuarine ecosystems.

We postulate that, in the absence of manatee grazing, H. wrightii is shaded out by the taller, more robust S. filiforme. Manatee grazing may help to maintain mixed-species seagrass beds.

FY 1999 $30,000
FY 2000 $37,000

K. Project Title and Summary:
Development of an adaptive management model to address the problem of manatee reliance on industrial warm water discharges.

Project is to develop population model(s), estimate parameters for model(s), and use model(s) in an adaptive management approach to manage manatees. Research results will be used to make recommendations about manatee

management with respect to such management actions as boat speed restrictions and power plant closing sequences.

Adaptive management seems to be an excellent tool for assessing and reducing the influence of industrial warm-water effluents, particularly power-generating plants, on manatee population dynamics. We are collaborating to develop several alternative models of manatee response to changes in power plant operations, based primarily on manatee photo identification and radio tracking studies conducted by our research team. Removal of thermal effluents can be viewed as a restoration action, but the short and long-term impacts on manatees are uncertain. We plan to work with plant industry personnel to design and test management strategies in an iterative process that, over time, optimizes the biological information obtained and improves management actions.

2000 Activities/Accomplishments

A basic model has been developed and estimation methodology for reproductive parameters has been developed. We are awaiting data to estimate parameters and will then implement modeling.

FY 2000 $0

L. Project Title and Summary:
Impacts of Hydrological Restoration on Three Estuarine Communities of the Southwest Florida Coasts and Associated Animal Inhabitants.

This 5-year study was initiated in FY 2000, as part of an integrated Center project to assess the impacts of hydrological restoration on estuarine communities of Southwest Florida. Given the manatee's reliance on freshwater and aquatic vegetation, we hypothesize that altered water management regimes will affect manatee distribution, relative abundance, habitat use, and movement patterns. We are also studying the distribution and relative abundance of manatees through the use of aerial strip-transect surveys, and the status of submerged aquatic vegetation in the Ten Thousand Islands region.

2000 Activities/Accomplishments

In June 2000, we initiated research on manatee movements through the use of radio telemetry and a data-logging Global Positioning System tag. Temperature, availability of fresh water, and spatial distribution of submerged aquatic vegetation, particularly seagrasses, are probably the most

important factors influencing manatee movement patterns along the southwest coast.

Mignucci-Giannoni, A.A., R.A. Montoya-Ospina, N.M. Jiménez-Marrero, M.A. Rodríguez-López, E.H. Williams, Jr., and R.K. Bonde. 2000. Manatee Mortality in Puerto Rico. Environmental Management 25(2):189-198.

Reid, J. P. 2000. Florida manatee now resident in the Bahamas. pp.7-8 in Sirenews.

FY 2000 $35,200

6. Southern sea otter

A. Project Title and Summary:
Population biology and behavior of sea otters.

The California sea otter population is presently listed as a threatened population under the ESA and depleted under the Act. While many northern populations have recovered to high levels or currently are growing rapidly, the California sea otter population has managed only a modest growth rate throughout most of this century and at present appears to be stable or declining. Furthermore, sea otter populations in western Alaska are in catastrophic decline, having reached densities of about one-tenth what they were in the early 1990s. The cause of the California sea otter's continued sluggish growth rate and more recent stasis are uncertain. The rapid decline rate of western Alaska populations appears to be a consequence of recent predation by killer whales.

A new study plan has been developed to focus more science relative to the demography of California sea otters due to recent population declines. The proposed work has two interrelated main objectives: (1) to monitor trends in the distribution and abundance of California sea otters; and (2) to determine the cause or causes for the current decline in population abundance.

This study has three broad goals: (1) to track sea otter population trends; (2) to determine the causes (demographically and environmentally) of trend changes; and (3) to develop standards (physiological, behavioral, and demographic) for assessing the status of populations. The purpose of the study is to document a broad suite of behavioral and life history characteristics in a population known to be below carrying capacity and currently growing at near the species' maximum rate. These studies are needed to understand how behavior and life history varies with population status, and to help evaluate the status of other populations, particularly the threatened southern sea otter population in California. The maximum rate of increase of sea otter populations is 17-20 percent yr-1. The sea otter population in Washington State has increased near this rate. In contrast, the sea otter population in central California has increased at an overall rate of about 4-5 percent yr-1.

1999 and 2000 Activities/ Accomplishments

1. The study plan has been approved after extensive peer, relevance, and animal care and use review.
2. Continuing sea otter abundance and distribution surveys have been completed.
3. Sea otter captures for implanting radio tracking devices and time-depth recorders will begin soon.

This research project will provide new and significant information on the natural history, behavior, and demography of sea otters. This information will be useful in developing conservation and management plans for the species throughout its range.

Research in California has shown that the growth rate of the sea otter population in central California recently has leveled off or begun to decline. The overall sluggish rate of growth and this more recent change are the result of changes in mortality, not reproduction or redistribution. Consistent with elevated mortality, the number of beach-cast carcasses has increased somewhat in recent years. Infectious disease and trauma appear to be the main contributors to this elevated mortality rate although there is no evidence that the incidence of infectious disease-related mortality has increased with the most recent population changes.

Studies in western Alaska have shown that the precipitous population declines are continuing unabated, are widespread over thousands of kilometers of shoreline, and are not due to infectious disease, toxicity, or starvation. Predation by killer whales has been found to be the likely cause of the declines. In Washington State, 79 sea otters have been captured so far during the study, 44 independent females, 16 independent males and 19 pups. Of these, 32 independent females, 15 independent males, and 9 pups were implanted with radio transmitters.

FY 1999	$150,000
FY 2000	$198,000
FY 2001	$609,000

B. Project Title and Summary:

Causes of southern sea otter mortality.

The southern sea otter received protection as a threatened species under the ESA in 1977. After its near extirpation in the late 19th century, the southern sea otter slowly expanded in numbers and range from a nucleus of animals at Big Sur, California, to currently range along approximately 200 miles of the central California coast. However, the growth rate of the southern sea otter population has been consistently lower (at 5 percent) than expanding northern sea otter populations (at 17-20 percent). In 1994, the growth rate in California was reduced to 0 percent and by 1998 a serious decline in population count was occurring, raising biologists' concerns that the population's recovery was in serious jeopardy.

A major factor limiting the population's growth appears to be an unusually high rate of mortality affecting both preweaning juveniles and adults. Prior to 1992, beach-cast carcasses were systematically collected and recorded but the causes were unknown for more than 50 percent of these deaths. The specific objective of this project is to document the causes of death in all southern sea otters found freshly dead along the California coast for a 5-year period, and thereafter to provide a continued lower level of monitoring for trends in the causes of death. The purpose of this project is to identify both overt and underlying factors detrimental to southern sea otter health; this information will be used as guidance for management strategies to reduce mortality, enhance the population's status, and facilitate recovery.

1999 and 2000 Activities/ Accomplishments

Five-year documentation of the causes of mortality in all freshly dead southern sea otters was completed in 1996. We found that California sea otters had an unexpectedly high rate of mortality from infectious diseases, and died from an unusually wide variety of infectious diseases. Forty percent of the otters we examined died from infectious diseases, 13 percent had miscellaneous conditions such as neoplasia or gastrointestinal obstructions, and in 19 percent, no cause of death could be determined. From 1997 through 1999, we continued to monitor causes of mortality at a reduced rate (every 4th freshly dead otter), and found that the proportionate causes of mortality had not changed substantially from observations in 1996.

We determined from a review of the literature and examination of archived tissues, as well as necropsy and parasitologic examination of recent carcasses, that gastrointestinal infections by the deleterious acanthocephalan parasite, Polymorphus sp., have increased in prevalence and severity over the past 20 years. From examination of two invertebrate species that are sea otter prey, we determined that both Emerita analoga and Blepharipoda occidentalis harbor intermediate forms of the parasite, Polymorphus sp., but the parasite was more prevalent and more numerous in Emerita. We had toxicologic analyses done on tissues from a small number of the dead adult otters to investigate the otters' exposure to two classes of aquatic contaminants with immunosuppressive properties, butylins, and organochlorine compounds, and found fairly high concentrations of butylins and PCBs in southern sea otter tissues in comparison with other marine species. Our toxicologic results indicate that southern sea otters are being exposed to some classes of immunosuppressive marine contaminants; however, the sample sizes analyzed to date are small and statistical correlations with the causes of mortality are inconclusive.

Article completed 4/28/1999: Thomas, N.J., L.H. Creekmore, R.A. Cole, and C.U. Meteyer. 1998. Emerging diseases in southern sea otters. p. 613 In: M.J. Mac, P.A. Opler, C.E. Puckett Haecker, P.D. Doran, editors. Status and Trends of the Nation's Biological Resources. 2 vols. U.S. Department of the Interior, U.S. Geological Survey, Reston, VA. 964 pp.

Presentation completed 4/9/1999: Thomas, N.J. 1999. Oral Progress Report to the Southern Sea Otter Recovery Team on Southern Sea Otter Necropsy Results and Environmental Contaminant Residues in the Tissues of Necropsied Otters, 1992-98. Southern Sea Otter Recovery Team Meeting, Monterey, CA, 8-10 April 1999.

Article completed 10/1/1999: Thomas, N.J., and L.H. Creekmore. 1999. Southern Sea Otter Health and Mortality: Questions Surrounding the Population Decline. The Otter Raft, Friends of the Sea Otter, Fall/Winter 1999 62:5-7.

Presentation completed 10/19/1999: Thomas, N.J. 1999. Southern Sea Otter Population Status/Possible Causes of the Ongoing Decline: Disease and Contaminants. Marine Mammal Commission Annual Meeting, Seaside, CA, 19-21 October 1999.

FY 1999 $0
FY 2000 $0

C. Project Title and Summary:
Population biology of the reintroduced Washington sea otter population.

The purpose of the study is to document a broad suite of behavioral and life history characteristics in a population known to be below carrying capacity and currently growing at or near the species' maximum rate. These studies are needed to understand how behavior and life history varies with population status, and to help evaluate the status of other populations, particularly the threatened southern sea otter population in California.

Efforts on sea otters along the Washington coast have paralleled efforts in California, providing a comparison in the recovery of two separate and distinct populations. The comparative study of demography of the Washington sea otter population is designed to identify critical demographic processes that may account for low population growth in California. Monitoring and survey of Washington sea otters has strong partnership support by the Service and Washington Department of Fish and Wildlife.

The maximum rate of increase of sea otter populations is 17-20 percent per year, and the sea otter population in Washington State has increased at near this rate. In contrast, the sea otter population in central California has increased at an overall rate of about 4-5 percent per year through 1994 but has declined in recent years.

The comparative study of demography of the Washington sea otter population is designed to identify critical demographic processes that may account for low population growth in California.

A variety of hypotheses concerning how population status influences diet, activity patterns, time budgets, distribution, movements, sexual segregation, agonistic interactions, survival and reproduction, and how these parameters vary among individuals of different age and sex are being examined. Radiotelemetry is used to compare foraging, social behavior, and demographic parameters among Washington, California, and Amchitka Island, Alaska, sea otter populations. The Washington population is considered to be well below its carrying capacity (K), the Amchitka Island Population is thought to have been at K for many years, and the status of the California population is uncertain. Radio transmitters, surgically implanted, are being used to locate the animals and measure the above listed parameters among these populations.

Research projects in Alaska and California have been completed or are ongoing under separate permits. In addition to the demographic study, the project also includes monitoring of population growth. This population is the result of translocations of sea otters from Alaska in 1969 and 1970 when a total of 59 sea otters were released on the outer coast of Washington State. Distribution and abundance of this population has been monitored by project biologists since 1977.

1999 and 2000 Activities/ Accomplishments

Results of this research will be used for comparison with results obtained from other demographic studies of sea otter populations from throughout the species' range. Results of population surveys are provided to stakeholders and will provide insight into the dynamics of population growth and range expansion for populations reoccupying historic habit from which they have been extirpated.

Weights of sea otters in Washington continue to be similar to those of otters captured in recently reoccupied areas in Alaska. Seven adult sea otters have been recaptured once each during this study, one male and six females. No significant changes in weight were found between the first and second capture. The 1999 population survey resulted in a total count of 605 sea otters. The population has continued to grow at an annual rate of about 11 percent since 1989.

1. Annual Washington sea otter population survey and reporting.
2. Development of Study Plan for "Environmental Contaminant Analysis of Sea Otters and Prey from Coastal Washington and the Washington Maritime NWR Complex."

Eleven sea otters were captured in 1998, 7 adult females, one adult male, and one pup. Nine were implanted with radio transmitters. The average adult female in 1998 weighed 24.3 kg (SE 0.90), not significantly different from the 1994, 1995, 1996, and 1997 averages of 24.9 (SE = 0.65), 22.9 (SE = 0.52), 23.9 kg (SE = 1.00), and 24.7 kg (SE = 1.17), respectively. The average weight of all adult females captured in Washington is 24.0 kg (SE = 0.35). Weights of sea otters in Washington continue to be similar to those of otters captured in recently reoccupied areas in Alaska. A result not unexpected since the translocation to Washington occurred only 30 years ago, the population remained at low levels for at least half that time, and only recently reoccupied much of the current range. Seven adult sea otters have been recaptured once each during this study, one male, and six females. No significant changes in weight were found between the first and second capture. Over 762 hours of activity data have been collected on instrumented animals.

We now have reproductive data for 23 females captured through 1997, which have produced 48 pups through 1998. The natality rate for adult females in Washington is 0.96-0.98, depending on method of calculation. These rates agree well with those from previously published studies in California. The 1999 population survey resulted in a total count of 605 sea otters. The population has continued to grow at an annual rate of about 11 percent since 1989.

FY 1999 $83,200
FY 2000 $92,000
FY 2001 $82,000

Enforcement

The Service's Division of Law Enforcement investigates known, alleged, or potential violations of the Act involving illegal take, importation, or exportation of marine mammals or their products for which the Service has statutory responsibility. In addition, the Division assists the NMFS by making apprehensions and conducting investigations in cases involving marine mammals and endangered and threatened species under that agency's jurisdiction. Results of these efforts are referred to the NMFS for its consideration and appropriate action. However, under an NMFS/Service Memorandum of Understanding, the Service retains authority over those investigations that involve endangered or threatened species under the jurisdiction of the Department. Violations are referred to the Department's Office of the Solicitor for civil action or the Department of Justice for criminal enforcement action.

Enforcement Activities in 1999

In the Service's Region 1, consisting of the west coast, Hawaii, and Pacific trust territories, Service wildlife inspectors are stationed at five designated ports and six border ports to closely monitor wildlife entering the country to detect the illegal importation of marine mammals and marine mammal products. Emphasis is placed on the designated wildlife ports of Seattle, Portland, San Francisco, Los Angeles, and Honolulu. Special border ports on the Washington/Idaho-Canada border, the California-Mexico border, and at Agana, Guam, continued to receive special attention. In 1999, Region 1 wildlife inspectors reported 32 incidents involving the illegal importation of marine mammals. The seizures involved products manufactured from seal, dolphin, whale, and walrus. Seventeen of the seizures involved Asian medicinals labeled to contain seal.

Protection of southern sea otters along the California coast remained a priority for Service special agents. During 1999, approximately 150 sea otters migrated south of Point Conception, Santa Barbara County, and remained in the near-shore waters of the Santa Barbara Channel from spring to early fall. The presence of this large number of otters in waters heavily used by the shell fishing industry has increased conflicts.

Agents continued to work closely with the California Department of Fish and Game (CDFG) in conducting offshore patrols to monitor the "live trap" fishery. Several State violations were identified during these patrols, resulting in the seizure of more than 70 illegal traps. Tentative findings from two Service-funded sea otter studies indicate otters can become caught in these traps. Unfortunately, a limited number of enforcement officers and the lack of suitable vessels preclude meaningful monitoring of the commercial fisheries located in the sea otter range.

The NMFS is conducting an observer program for incidental "take" of porpoise in a northern Monterey Bay gill net fishery. Observers for the study documented the drowning of a sea otter in their gill nets this year.

Two other sea otter deaths in Monterey Bay were attributed to collisions with boat propellers. The area where the dead sea otters were found was Elk Horn Slough near Moss Landing, California. This is an area where many sea otters have been observed in the narrow slough. Boat activity in the slough in excess of the 5-mph speed limit has been documented. Increased enforcement of the boat speed limit and intermittent presence of Service agents should help prevent otter deaths in this area.

Two sea otters were found to have died of gunshot wounds in California during 1999. One of the otters was found near Half Moon Bay, and the other otter was found at Pescadero State Beach, south of Half Moon Bay. No suspects have been identified.

Service agents participated in a multiagency law enforcement task force along the central coast of California aimed at reducing human harassment of elephant seals. Major haul-out areas for these seals are becoming tourist attractions. Harassment of the seals and related State violations were documented.

One noteworthy case investigated by Service agents involved Lan Chile Airlines, which transported eight live sea lions from Uruguay to the United States. Upon arrival at Los Angeles, Service wildlife inspectors determined that five of the sea lions were dead and three were severely dehydrated. The Service coordinated with the NMFS to determine if NMFS requirements had been met. The trainer, who was traveling with the animals, confirmed they were circus animals valued at approximately $40,000. The investigation revealed that the animals were shipped from Uruguay to Chile, and finally to Los Angeles. The shipping containers, as well as the temperature in the hold of the airplane, did not meet the standards established by 50 CFR Part 14 for humane shipping. The dead animals were necropsied by the Los Angeles County Museum, which found the cause of death to be excessive heat and dehydration. The three surviving animals were temporarily held at the Marine Mammal Care Center and were later authorized reexportation (by the NMFS) to the shipper in Uruguay. A Violation Notice for inhumane shipping was issued to Lan Chile Airlines.

Wildlife inspectors at the port of San Francisco "tagged" 19 sport hunted polar bear trophies imported from Canada. Wildlife inspectors affix a locking tag with a unique serial number to the hide and permanently mark any bear skulls included in the shipment. The importation of sport hunted polar bear trophies is legal, provided the importation is authorized by a Canadian CITES export permit and an import permit from the Service's Division of Management Authority.

Investigation of a subject offering a polar bear skin for sale in Washington State led to the abandonment of the hide, with no penalty assessed.

In the Service's southeastern Region, Region 4, which includes the State of Florida, protecting the endangered manatee population was a major focus of enforcement efforts during 1999. Death by boat strike has historically been a significant cause of manatee mortality, and boating is "big business" in Florida. In 1996, there were 714,000 registered boats in Florida, and 60 out of 416 manatee deaths (14 percent) were attributed to boat strikes. In 1997, the percentage of boat-related mortality rose to 22 percent (54 out of 246 deaths), while in 1998, boat-related mortality increased to 27 percent (66 out of 243 deaths). The State of Florida currently estimates that there are over 800,000 registered boats in the State; when these vessels are combined with transient craft, the total reaches a million boats a year utilizing Florida

waters. In an effort to reduce manatee mortality, the Service and the State of Florida have established boating speed zones in areas used by manatees where boat strike deaths are frequent. To secure compliance with the speed zones, Service special agents organized and coordinated manatee protection task forces with the assistance of officers from the USCG, Florida Marine Patrol (FMP), National Wildlife Refuge System, and Sheriffs' Departments. In 1999, these task forces apprehended 799 boaters for speeding in manatee protection zones. (Note: As of March 2000, 551 of these cases have been adjudicated, collecting fines totaling $55,220.) Additionally, special agents processed 697 manatee speed zone violation cases in Federal court that were referred to the Service for prosecution by the USCG.

In the Service's Region 7, comprised entirely of the State of Alaska, special agents continued their aggressive, proactive efforts to find a balance between effective law enforcement and the very real needs of subsistence hunters in remote Alaskan villages. Agents participated in meetings of Native organizations, such as the Eskimo Walrus Commission (EWC), and in meetings in rural villages standing shoulder to shoulder with local leaders and subsistence hunters. These efforts amount to a substantial and important law enforcement effort that is not readily measurable in cases made or arrest statistics.

While encouraging compliance with existing laws, agents are often faced with the reality that existing regulations do not adequately address situations unique to Alaska. The Service in Alaska continues to face challenges in enforcing provisions of the Native exemption under the Act in a number of areas, such as Native handicrafts and tagging requirements.

A task force operation in Alaska looked at reported violations by marine mammal registered agents and tanneries. Service special agents inspected all 19 facilities located in Alaska, finding violations at nearly every location ranging from failure to keep required records to illegal sale of marine mammals. Several permittees were cited with violation notices ranging from $250 to $500, and agents are following up on leads that were developed. Additional charges are expected.

In another case, Barrow police officers discovered a raw polar bear hide at a residence while serving a drug search warrant. Service agents were called in to investigate this possible violation of the

Act. Thus far, agents have been able to determine that the hide was obtained as part of a drug transaction; this investigation continues.

In Anchorage, Service special agents received a complaint that raw walrus ivory was being offered for sale during a street fair. A special agent made covert contact with two individuals selling handicrafts to tourists. When the individuals offered to sell the agent three raw walrus head mounts, the agent identified himself, seized necessary evidence, and presented the case to the U.S. Attorney for prosecution. Subsequently, one of the individuals, who was the owner of the head mounts, pleaded guilty, was fined $500, and forfeited a head mount. The man's adult son was successfully prosecuted the year before for selling a polar bear hide to a Service undercover agent.

A Ketchikan gift shop owner was investigated for selling polar bear fur to tourists. He subsequently paid a $500 fine.

Enforcement Activities in 2000

During 2000, wildlife inspectors in Region 1 identified and seized 37 shipments of marine mammal products at the designated ports of entry, special border ports, and Guam. The items seized included whale bones collected by tourists along the beaches of Mexico, Asian medicinals containing walrus and seal parts, whale meat and teeth, and walrus carvings imported through the international airports. A total of 18 polar bear trophies from Canada were imported and cleared by Service wildlife inspectors in Region 1 last year. The absence of violations associated with polar bear trophies may be, in part, the result of Service outreach efforts at the Safari Club International annual convention, held each year in Nevada. Service special agents and wildlife inspectors, as well as personnel from the Service's Division of Management Authority (the Office responsible for issuing trophy import permits), staff a booth at the convention and answer numerous questions concerning the requirements for importation of hunting trophies, a significant number of which are specific to polar bears.

In southern California, two sea otter deaths from shooting were investigated during 2000. The first sea otter shooting occurred on April 15 just south of Morro Bay, San Luis Obispo County, where the animal was found freshly killed (within 10 hours of death). Necropsy was performed and the bullet fragments were removed and sent to the

Clark R. Bavin National Fish and Wildlife Forensics Laboratory (Forensics Lab) for ballistics examination. Several leads were investigated by Service special agents and CDFG officers, but no suspects have been identified. The second sea otter shooting occurred in Monterey Bay, Monterey County, on September 20 with the animal found dead on the beach. The otter was X-rayed and necropsied, and the bullet fragments were also sent to the Forensics Lab. A reward has been offered for the arrest and conviction of the subjects who did the shooting. Thus far, no leads have developed.

The conflicts between sea otters and the shell-fish fishery in the Santa Barbara Channel area, and the live trap and gill net fisheries along California's central coast continue. Service special agents participated in joint enforcement patrols with the CDFG in these areas. Particular emphasis was placed on monitoring sea otters in the near-shore waters south of Point Conception, where the animals continued a seasonal migration south from their main range. This pattern of behavior places the otters in direct conflict with the sea urchin harvest and has been the subject of a growing controversy between the Service and commercial fishing interests in southern California. The CDFG closed the gill net fishery in the near-shore waService special agents stationed in
Washington State closed two investigations that had been opened in 1999. One case involved the seizure and abandonment of a polar bear rug valued at $1,200, and the other case involved the abandonment of one walrus oosik (i.e., penis bone).

Agents in that State also completed two additional investigations. In the first case special agents acted on a tip received from a major airline after a routine X-ray of passenger luggage revealed a walrus skull and tusks. The subject of the investigation had purchased the walrus "head mount" ters between Point Sal and Point Conception in an effort to protect otters and marine birds, which were drowning in the nets. Service special agents have assisted in several joint patrols in the closed area.

Service special agents also continued to provide assistance to the NMFS and the California Highway Patrol in Monterey County by monitoring and controlling large numbers of people who visit a small stretch of beach to view a major elephant seal "haul out" area. In addition to harassment of the elephant seals, the crowds create a major hazard to traffic along a narrow section of the coast highway.

Service special agents stationed in Washington State closed two investigations that had been opened in 1999. One case involved the seizure and abandonment of a polar bear rug valued at $1,200, and the other case involved the abandonment of one walrus oosik (i.e., penis bone).

Agents in that State also completed two additional investigations. In the first case special agents acted on a tip received from a major airline after a routine X-ray of passenger luggage revealed a walrus skull and tusks. The subject of the investigation had purchased the walrus "head mount" from an Alaska Native living in Dutch Harbor, Alaska. The subject was offered the opportunity to abandon the walrus head mount to the Government, which he subsequently did, and the case was closed. In another case, a polar bear hide was pawned at a pawn shop. An investigation determined that the person who pawned the hide received it from a homeless person who exchanged the hide for a place to stay. The hide was subsequently abandoned to the Government and has been donated to the Idaho Fish and Game Department for use in public outreach efforts.

Region 1 wildlife inspectors continue to participate in a multiagency task force designed to interdict the importation of illegal drugs and other controlled substances, which often include products containing, or labeled to contain, parts of marine mammals. Numerous Federal, State, and local agencies with various regulatory responsibilities plan and conduct operations such as "walk through" inspections of shops and warehouses known to traffic in these products, increased baggage inspection of airlines flights with a history of violations, and increased examination of international mail, including the use of a wildlife scent detection dog.

Protecting the endangered manatee population continued to be a major focus of law enforcement efforts during 2000 as boat strike manatee mortalities showed no tendency to decline. Coordinated efforts involving manatee protection task forces continued to enforce established boating speed zones as a means to reduce manatee deaths. During 2000, these task forces issued 1,538 Violation Notices (i.e., tickets) to boaters for speeding in manatee protection zones. (Note: As of March 2001, more than 1,100 of these cases had been adjudicated, collecting fines totaling $91,195. Additionally, special agents processed 687 manatee speed zone violation cases in Federal court that were referred to the Service for prosecution

by the Coast Guard. As of March 2001, the court has adjudicated 167 of these cases, collecting $16,700 in fines).

In Alaska in 2000, special agents continued their enforcement efforts while considering the needs of subsistence hunters in remote Alaskan villages. Agents, in conjunction with representatives of the EWC and Service biologists, met on numerous occasions with village leaders and subsistence hunters to encourage compliance with the regulations, especially wasteful take provisions.

Agents in Alaska investigated a Kodiak charter boat operator who, under the guise of a marine mammal registered agent permit, was killing sea otters and seals from his 60-foot boat and marketing them. This investigation documented the unlawful take of over 100 animals between November 1999 and March 2000. A Federal grand jury investigation is ongoing.

Wildlife inspectors for Alaska were involved in ten cases at Anchorage's Import/Export Office during 2000. The cases resulted in the seizure of walrus ivory, seal pelts, and sperm whale teeth.

Permits and Registrations

The Act prohibits the take or import of marine mammals and marine mammal products. Exceptions may be made under permits for scientific research, public display, import of sport-hunted trophies of polar bears taken in Canada, photography for educational or commercial purposes, or to enhance the survival or recovery of a species or stock. Another exception streamlines the permitting process for conducting scientific research by allowing a General Authorization for activities that may result in the take of marine mammals by Level B harassment in the course of bona fide scientific research.

The Act provides an exemption to the take prohibitions for Alaska Natives for subsistence purposes and to create and sell Native handicrafts. In order to enable marine mammal hides to be tanned and to facilitate trade of products among Alaska Natives, registered agent/tannery permits may be issued to non-Alaska Natives (i.e., persons other than Alaskan Indians, Eskimos, or Aleuts). Registered agents may purchase and sell raw parts and tanned skins from and to Alaska Natives or other registered agents, provided that only authentic Alaska Native handicrafts or clothing are purchased or sold in interstate commerce. Raw parts may be transferred (not sold) to registered tanners for further processing. Registered tanners may transfer (not sell) parts received for processing to Alaska Natives or registered agents only.

Section 104 of the Act authorizes the Director of the Service, acting on behalf of the Secretary of the Interior, to issue permits for the activities identified above. Applicable provisions are found in Title 50 of the Code of Federal Regulations— 50 CFR 18.23(d) for registered agent/tannery permits, 50 CFR 18.30 for sport-hunted polar bear imports, and 50 CFR 18.31 for scientific research or public display permits. Regulations will be developed for a General Authorization for activities that may result in the take of marine mammals by Level B harassment in the course of bona fide scientific research and for issuance of permits for enhancement of the survival or recovery of a species or stock, photography for educational or commercial purposes, and beached or stranded marine mammals that are designated as non-releasable under the Act.

Permit Activities in 1999

During 1999, the Service finalized regulations proposed in 1998, approving two additional polar bear populations, that allowed for the issuance of permits under section 104(c)(5)(A) of the Act to import personal sport-hunted polar bear trophies taken in Canada. Also during the year, four new permits for scientific research were issued and four were amended. In addition, 3 permits were issued for public display, 1 permit was issued for enhancement, 16 parties either registered or renewed their registration as agents and/or tanneries, and 143 permits were issued for the import of sport-hunted polar bear trophies from Canada.

Scientific Research Permits

1. Permit 009526, issued December 16, 1999, through December 18, 2004, to the NMFS, Marine Mammal Health and Stranding Response Program; amended NMFS Permit 932-1489 to include take of all species of the Order Sirenia, and walrus, polar bear, sea otter, and marine otter for the purposes of scientific research and enhancement. The activities include: (1) collection, transport, import, and export of cadavers or tissue and fluid samples for analysis; (2) take of stranded or distressed animals; and (3) salvage of specimens from dead animals.

2. Permit 010249, issued June 28, 1999, through June 25, 2004, to the Hubbs-Sea World Research Institute to take (harass) captive West Indian manatees that are undergoing rehabilitation, for scientific research to determine the method of manatee entanglement in (simulated) fishing gear and to devise appropriate mitigation.

3. Permit 011638, issued September 3, 1999, through December 31, 2002, to the USGS/BRD, amended the NMFS Permit 930-1486 to include take of southern sea otters during aerial surveys for the purpose of scientific research.

4. Permit 017419, newly issued October 21, 1999, and amended November 10, 1999, through November 9, 2000, to Darlene Ketten, Woods Hole Oceanographic Institution, for scientific research of dugongs as part of a study on how the structural elements of marine mammal ears contribute to underwater hearing. The permit was amended to correct the number of biological specimens authorized for import from dead, stranded individuals or collected from aboriginal hunts in Australia.

5. Permit 717015, amended jointly with the NMFS January 12, 1999, through January 6, 2003, to the Natural History Museum of Los Angeles County to import, reimport, export, and reexport salvaged material from dead Cetacea, Pinnipedia, Sirenia, polar bear, sea otter, and marine otter for the purposes of scientific research and public display. The permit was amended to include endangered species authorization inadvertently omitted at the time of last renewal.

6. Permit 766818, amended April 19, 1999, through February 7, 2002, to the USGS/BRD, for scientific research of Alaska sea otters and southern sea otters. The permit was amended to add authorized personnel.

7. Permit 791721, amended December 15, 1999, through December 31, 2004, to the U.S. Geological Survey, Sirenia Project, to take West Indian manatees for scientific research. The permit was amended to increase the allowable number of implants of passive integrated transponder (PIT) tags and number of animals for tail notching.

Public Display Permits

1. Permit 012337, issued September 10, 1999, through September 7, 2004, to the Aquarium of the Americas to use sea otter pelts (Enhydra lutris kenyoni), as provided by the Service, in an education/conservation program for public display.

2. Permit 838026, issued August 16, 1999, through August 15, 2000, to Ferris State University to import a polar bear from the Northwest Territories, Canada, donated to the University for public display.

3. Permit 844696, issued April 9, 1999, through April 6, 2004, to the Alaska Zoo, Anchorage, Alaska, to take one female polar bear that was recovered as an orphaned cub in Alaska for public display.

Enhancement Permits

1. Permit 001425, issued November 10, 1999, through November 10, 2000, to the Dallas World Aquarium to import two orphaned/abandoned manatee calves (Trichechus manatus) from Venezuela for enhancement of the survival of the species.

Registered Agent/Tannery Permits

1. Permit 006762, Last Frontier Taxidermy, Anchorage, Alaska, was registered as an agent on May 26, 1999.

2. Permit 008188, Roger Lehrman-Bon, Eagle River, Alaska, was registered as an agent on March 3, 1999.

3. Permit 011100, Shadow Mountain Trading Company, Ketchikan, Alaska, was registered as an agent on June 7, 1999.

4. Permit 011401, the Great Alaskan Tannery, Wasilla, Alaska, was registered as a tannery on May 24, 1999.

5. Permit 011438, Ikam'aq Tanning, Cordova, Alaska, was registered as a tannery on May 12, 1999.

6. Permit 012275, Patrick Malone, Eagle River, Alaska, was registered as an agent on June 11, 1999.

7. Permit 019560, Sea-Tac Taxidermy, Edgewood, Washington, was registered as a tannery on December 13, 1999.

8. Permit 019705, Darren Byler, Kodiak, Alaska, was registered as an agent on December 3, 1999.

9. Permit 681597, renewed the registration of George Kritchen, Cordova, Alaska, as an agent on February 24, 1999.

10. Permit 697867, renewed the registration of Bob McConnell, Jr., Anchorage, Alaska, as an agent on March 22, 1999.

11. Permit 704234, renewed the registration of Bears Den, Inc., Olympia, Washington, as an agent on November 12, 1999.

12. Permit 797559, renewed the registration of Chukotka-Alaska, Inc., Nome, Alaska, as an agent on February 19, 1999.

13. Permit 799354, renewed the registration of the Ivory House, Anchorage, Alaska, as an agent on July 16, 1999.

14. Permit 799658, renewed the registration of Prince of Wales Taxidermy and Fur, Craig, Alaska, as an agent on July 16, 1999.

15. Permit 827696, renewed the registration of Tall Tale Taxidermy and Furs, Ward Cove, Alaska, as an agent on November 16, 1999.

16. Permit 831167, renewed the registration of Shawn Mc Crary, Palmer, Alaska, as an agent/tannery on February 23, 1999.

Polar Bear Trophy Import Permits

Approved Populations	Number of Permits Issued
Southern Beaufort Sea	16
Northern Beaufort Sea	8
Viscount Melville	0
McClintock Channel	10
Western Hudson Bay	2
Lancaster Sound	105
Norwegian Bay	1

Deferred Populations (Pre-Amendment ONLY)	Number of Permits Issued
Queen Elizabeth Islands	0
Kane Basin	0
Baffin Bay	0
Gulf of Boothia	0
Foxe Basin	0
Davis Strait	1
Southern Hudson Bay	0

Permit Activities in 2000

During 2000, 4 new permits were issued for scientific research, 5 permits were amended, and 1 was renewed; 1 new permit was issued for public display and 1 permit was amended; 6 parties either registered or renewed their registration as agents and/or tanneries, and 76 permits were issued for the import of sport-hunted polar bear trophies from Canada. The polar bear assessment report was not completed during the year as originally anticipated due to other priorities. It's completion and publication was planned for 2001.

Scientific Research Permits

1. Permit 001145, renewed July 25, 2000, through July 25, 2002, to the Mote Marine Laboratory for scientific research of captive-held West Indian manatees to determine the cause(s) of elevated creatinine levels that occur when rehabilitated manatees are released into the wild.

2. Permit 010370, issued January 28, 2000, through January 25, 2002, to the Monterey Bay Aquarium for scientific research of captive southern sea otters that are undergoing rehabilitation, to develop and test an enhanced radio tagging technique.

3. Permit 017891, issued jointly with the NMFS May 16, 2000, through March 31, 2005, to the University of California Santa Cruz, Museum of Natural History Collections, to acquire and import/export marine mammal specimens of the Orders Cetacea, Pinnipedia, and Sirenia for the purposes of scientific research and for deposit into a museum collection.

4. Permit 021423, issued February 24, 2000, through February 21, 2005, to Zachary Sharp, University of New Mexico, to import cross-sections of canine teeth of Atlantic walrus (Odobenus rosmarus rosmarus) for scientific research for a preliminary analysis to determine if tooth cementum shows significant variations in stable isotopes of carbon, nitrogen, and lead.

5. Permit 033974, issued November 28, 2000, through November 26, 2005 to the Florida Museum of Natural History for scientific research on manatees (Trichechus spp.) to conduct stable isotopic analyses of tooth fragments taken from existing museum specimens or naturally shed from captive individuals to determine the the diet composition in order to compare the diets of modern and ancient manatees.

6. Permit 766818, amended October 27, 2000, through February 7, 2002, to the USGS/BRD for scientific research of Alaska and southern sea otters. The permit was amended to include the collection of liver biopsy samples to determine estimates of contaminants exposure.

7. Permit 773494, amended November 29, 2000, through July 22, 2003, to the Florida Fish and Wildlife Conservation Commission, Florida Marine Research Center, to take West Indian manatees for scientific research. The permit was amended to include authorization to conduct a preliminary study for one winter season at the Big Bend canal on the use of a remote-controlled floating scanner to scan PIT tags on manatees.

8. Permit 777239, amended March 9, 2000, through December 31, 2002, to the Western Ecological Research Center, USGS (WERC), to take Alaska sea otters for scientific research. The permit was amended to allow the take of an additional 33 sea otters in order to continue studies of the species' ability to reoccupy historical habitats and to continue sampling individuals to assess contaminant loads.

9. Permit 834406, amended April 3, 2000, through November 25, 2002, to the Mote Marine Laboratory, for scientific research of captive-held West Indian manatees. The permit was amended to include the opportunistic collection of blood from manatees undergoing rehabilitation at authorized institutions outside the State of Florida.

10. Permit 837923, amended January 12, 2000, through January 12, 2005, to the New College of the University of South Florida, for scientific research of captive-held West Indian manatees. The permit was amended to include a study to test the manatee's ability to use its sense of touch, without visual aid, to understand its environment.

Public Display Permits

1. Permit 014704, amended March 16, 2000, through March 16, 2005, to the Toledo Zoological Gardens, to import a captive-born polar bear from Germany for public display. The permit was amended to substitute a captive-born polar bear from Belgium.

2. Permit 032510, issued November 24, 2000, through November 21, 2005, to the Chicago Zoological Park (Brookfield Zoo), to import a captive-born polar bear for public display.

Registered Agent/Tannery Permits

1. Permit 022474, registered Virgil Schumacher, Yakutat, Alaska, as a tannery on February 4, 2000.

2. Permit 024572, registered Megagem, Anchorage, Alaska, as an agent on May 8, 2000.

3. Permit 027560, registered W.D. Taxidermy, Wasilla, Alaska, as an agent/ tannery on June 6, 2000.

4. Permit 812648, renewed the registration of Elizabeth West, Sitka Fur & Leather, Sitka, Alaska, as an agent on February 24, 2000.

5. Permit 822365, registered Ron Alleva, Grubstake Auction, Anchorage, Alaska, as an agent on February 29, 2000.

6. Permit 839290, renewed the registration of Duane Edward Hill, Alaska Auction Company, Anchorage, Alaska, as an agent on March 23, 2000.

7. Permit 011401, the Great Alaskan Tannery, Wasilla, Alaska; registered tannery permit was revoked on April 24, 2000.

8. Permit 799354, the Ivory House, Anchorage, Alaska; registered agent permit was revoked on June 14, 2000.

Polar Bear Trophy Import Permits

Approved Populations	Number of Permits Issued
Southern Beaufort Sea	18
Northern Beaufort Sea	9
Viscount Melville	0
McClintock Channel	14
Western Hudson Bay	2
Lancaster Sound	31
Norwegian Bay	1

Deferred Populations (Pre-AmendmentONLY)	Number of Permits Issued
Queen Elizabeth Islands	0
Kane Basin	0
Baffin Bay	0
Gulf of Boothia	0
Foxe Basin	0
Davis Strait	1
Southern Hudson Bay	0

International Activities

United States-Russia Environmental Agreement: Marine Mammal Project

The Agreement between the Government of the United States of America and the Government of the Russian Federation on Cooperation in the Field of Protection of the Environment and Natural Resources was signed on June 23, 1994, and supersedes the previous Agreement between the United States and the Soviet Union of May 23, 1972. The Service coordinates Area V of the Agreement for the U.S. side. Over nearly 30 years, the Agreement has served as an effective instrument for facilitating the exchange of scientific data and organization of cooperative field research by U.S. and Russian biologists.

The Service, in partnership with the USGS/BRD, the NMFS, the State of Alaska, and colleagues from universities and nongovernmental organizations, collaborated with the Russian State Fisheries Committee, Russian Academy of Sciences, and Russian State Committee for Environmental Protection in conducting marine mammal management and research activities in 1999. Under the auspices of the bilateral marine mammal project, nine U.S. specialists traveled to Russia, while six Russians traveled to the United States for jointly sponsored activities.

Throughout 1999, the two sides remained in contact on efforts to conclude a proposed United States-Russia Agreement on the Conservation and Management of the Alaska-Chukotka Polar Bear Population.

An American polar bear biologist traveled to Chukotka, Russia, in the spring for several weeks at the invitation of the Union of Marine Mammal Hunters for discussions on utilizing traditional ecological knowledge to identify polar bear habitat use.

In spring, the NMFS hosted two Russian biologists for two weeks in California for continued collaboration on bowhead (Balaena mysticetus) and gray (Eschrichtius robustus) whale research.

The NMFS National Marine Mammal Laboratory in Seattle, Washington, hosted two Russian specialists for several weeks in the spring for the continuation of Northern fur seal studies and analysis of data.

Polar bears in Cape Lisburne

Gerry Atwell/USFWS

A NMFS biologist and colleague traveled to Russia for two weeks in late summer to coordinate field research with Russian scientists on bowhead and gray whales around Sakhalin Island.

The Service hosted one Russian biologist in Alaska for three weeks in spring to participate in Pacific walrus harvest monitoring training and to gain field experience. The EWC hosted additional harvest monitors from Russia who received training.

One Russian was hosted in Alaska for one month in summer by Service to take part in an ice-edge research cruise to study the composition and productivity of walrus herds in the Chukchi Sea.

Six Americans attended the 15th Marine Mammals Working Group Meeting under Area V of the United States-Russia Environmental Agreement. The meeting was held in November 1999 in Kamchatka, Russia.

The Aleutian sea otter population decline was identified as a priority issue and the Service has been active in identifying funding sources to support the continuation of sea otter population surveys in Russia in the Commander Islands and Kamchatka Peninsula. Having Russian scientists continue their efforts in documenting sea otter population trends would provide a more complete picture of the extent of the population decline in the Aleutians.

In January-February 2000, the Service hosted four Russian polar bear specialists in Anchorage, Alaska, for 12 days to finalize the proceedings of a workshop to design polar bear den survey methods and discuss population density assessment techniques in connection with aerial surveys in the Bering and Chukchi Seas.

For one week in March, the Service hosted three Russian specialists in Anchorage to conduct consultations on the final text of the Agreement between the Government of the United States of America and the Government of the Russian Federation on the Conservation and Management of the Alaska-Chukotka Polar Bear Population.

One Russian researcher visited the United States for two months in March-May 2000 for cooperative Steller sea lion studies with the Alaska SeaLife Center in Seward, Alaska. Data collected in 1998-99 via remote video monitoring on Chiswell Island, Alaska, were analyzed and compared with data collected in Russia on Medniy Island.

In March 2000, the Service and USGS/BRD hosted a workshop in Anchorage, Alaska, to evaluate various techniques and approaches to estimate the size and trend of the Pacific walrus population. Workshop participants included U.S. and Russian experts in walrus biology and survey design, subsistence hunters, and resource managers. Previous efforts to survey the Pacific walrus population were reviewed and problems that were encountered in designing and conducting those surveys identified. The group also summarized survey conditions by season and assessed potential tools and techniques for surveying walrus populations.

In May one Russian researcher from Kamchatka visited the National Marine Mammal Laboratory (NMML) in Seattle, Washington, for 2.5 weeks of collaboration on the analysis of data on northern fur seals from both Russian and U.S. populations.

Two Russian specialists from Kamchatka were hosted by the Alaska SeaLife Center and participated in one month of Steller sea lion studies in June-July in the Aleutian Islands and Gulf of Alaska.

In July-August two U.S. cetacean researchers visited eastern Russia for one month of collaboration on studies of the Okhotsk-Korea population of gray whales.

One Russian researcher from Kamchatka visited the United States for three weeks in July-August for studies of harbor seals in Alaska. The research involved the catching of harbor seals and attachment of radio transmitters near Nanvak Bay (north Bristol Bay), Alaska.

In 2000, the second season of bilateral walrus harvest monitoring occurred in walrus hunting villages in Chukotka, Russia. Details are presented in the Pacific Walrus section on following pages.

One Russian researcher from Vladivostok visited the United States for three weeks in August-September to participate in population studies of northern fur seals in the Pribilof Islands, Alaska.

In September 2000, two NMFS/NMML staff members attended the conference "Marine Mammals of the Palearctic" in Archangelsk, Russia, hosted by the Russian Interdepartmental Ichthyological Commission and the Russian Marine Mammal Council.

Two Russian researchers visited the United States for two months in September-November to collaborate with USGS at the Alaska Biological Science Center in Anchorage in assessing sea ice habitat parameters and their effect on the movements and behavior of polar bears and walruses. The work involves the classification of methods for monitoring Arctic sea ice using Okean-series SLR/ passive microwave instruments. Additionally, the Moscow-based researchers met with the Director and staff of the Science and Applied Technology Office of the U.S. National

Ice Center in Washington, D.C., and discussed their evaluations and ice mapping methods.

On October 16, 2000, six Russian Government and Native representatives attended the signing of the "Agreement Between the Government of the United States of America and the Government of the Russian Federation on the Conservation and Management of the Alaska-Chukotka Polar Bear Population" in Washington, D.C. The Agreement, signed by David Sandalow, Assistant Secretary of State and Yuriy Ushakov, Russian Ambassador to the United States, is designed to strengthen the management and research efforts for this distinct population of polar bears. The Agreement fulfills the spirit and intent of the 1973 International Agreement on the Conservation of Polar Bears to which the U.S. and Russia, along with Canada, Norway, and Denmark (for Greenland), are Contracting Parties. Additional details appear on following pages in the Polar Bear section of this report.

One Russian researcher from Moscow, studying sea ice habitat delineation, visited the United States for 12 days during October-November 2000 to attend a meeting of the principal investigators of the International Arctic Research Center-Cooperative Institute for Arctic Research (IARC-CIFAR) at the University of Alaska in Fairbanks. Cooperation is under activity 02.05-7105 "Application of Contemporary Technology in Studies of Large Mammals" of Area V of the United States-Russia Agreement on Cooperation in the Field of Environmental Protection.

From November 14-16, 2000, six Russian scientists from Kamchatka and Moscow met with U.S. colleagues in Monterey, California, to attend the 7th biennial U.S.-Russia Sea Otter Workshop to share information on sea otters, to discuss the implications of recent population declines, to identify needed research and management projects, and to develop a protocol for information exchange and shared projects between the United States and Russia to be conducted over the following two years. Planning for this workshop was initiated in 1999. Thirty-five papers presented at the meeting addressed population status and trends, health and genetics, conservation, management, and ecology of sea otters. Participants included biologists from Japan, Russia, and the United States. The Aleutian sea otter population decline was identified as a priority issue and a special session was held to discuss research and

management directions for the future. Recommendations included: continued monitoring of the Commander Islands in Russia (as a possible control site for comparison with the Aleutians), continued work at existing long-term monitoring sites in the western and central Aleutians and additional sites in the eastern Aleutians, and the need for studies to address the cause of the decline in greater detail.

Status Reports for 1999 and 2000

Stock Assessments

The 1994 amendments to the Act require the Service and the NMFS, in consultation with Scientific Review Groups created by the amendments, to prepare, periodically review, and revise stock assessment reports for all stocks of marine mammals occurring in U.S. waters. These stock assessments are intended to provide information for making management decisions to address the incidental take of marine mammals in commercial fisheries. Stock assessment reports use the best available information on population size and productivity to calculate the PBR level that the population could sustain, and compare the PBR with estimates of annual human-caused mortality to assess the status of the stock. Pursuant to this provision of the statute, stocks are either designated as strategic or non-strategic. A strategic stock is one that: is listed as threatened or endangered under the ESA, or depleted under the Act; is declining and is likely to be listed as threatened under the ESA within the foreseeable future; or is a stock with a level of direct human-caused mortality that exceeds its PBR.

In October 1995, we completed and released our initial stock assessments for Pacific walrus, northern sea otters in Alaska and Washington State, two stocks of polar bears, southern sea otter, and two stocks of West Indian manatees. For Pacific walrus, based upon the best available information on population size, productivity, and estimates of human-caused mortality, the stock was given a nonstrategic determination. In 1998, the Pacific walrus stock assessment was revised and finalized to include new information on fisheries and harvest-related mortality. In the absence of new population data, no changes were proposed to the estimated PBR level. The inclusion of the latest fisheries and harvest information resulted in a slightly lower estimate of average annual human-caused mortality, therefore, the designation of this stock remains nonstrategic. During review of the Pacific walrus stock assessment report, conservation organizations and members of the scientific community raised concerns that the population data used to calculate safe removal levels were becoming outdated. The next revision of the Pacific walrus stock assessment was conducted in 2001.

northern sea otter in Alaska identified one Statewide stock. It concluded that, based upon the best scientific information available on population size, productivity, and estimates of human-caused mortality, the stock was nonstrategic. In 1998, based on new information on fisheries, stock identity, and harvest related mortality, we developed three draft revised stock assessments to denote separate stocks in southeast, southcentral, and southwest Alaska. This delineation was based on genetics, morphology and geographic separation. All three stocks were designated as nonstrategic.

Following a 90-day public review and comment period for the draft revised stock assessments, a decision was made not to finalize the documents. At that time, The Alaska Sea Otter and Steller Sea Lion Commission (TASSC) objected to the delineation of three separate sea otter stocks, stating that the science used to differentiate the stocks was deficient. In accordance with section 117 of the Act, their objection required a formal proceeding on the record to resolve the issue. In August 1999, TASSC withdrew their objection based on a Memorandum of Agreement with the Service to cooperatively gather and analyze additional genetic information to reevaluate the proposed stock structure, as well as finalize information referenced in the 1998 draft stock assessments. One analysis of mitochondrial and nuclear DNA completed in November 2000 supports the identification of multiple sea otter stocks within Alaska. Also in the interim since the draft stock assessment reports were prepared, the journal Marine Mammal Science accepted for publication the paper that detailed the rationale for multiple stocks. The Service expects to revise the northern sea otter stock assessment in 2001.

Currently, as identified in our 1995 and subsequent revised final 1998 stock assessments, there are two recognized polar bear population stocks in Alaska: the Southern Beaufort Sea population, which is shared with Canada; and the Chukchi/Bering Seas population, which is shared with Russia. Recent cluster analysis of radiotelemetry data on female polar bears has indicated that there may be three functional stocks in Alaska: the Southern Beaufort Sea, the western Chukchi Sea, and the eastern Chukchi Sea. Until more information is

available to validate the discreteness of the eastern Chukchi Sea population, management decisions will continue to include this stock with the Southern Beaufort Sea stock. Information on population size is either outdated or unavailable for all stocks. Future polar bear population survey and inventory projects over remote areas of the arctic are needed but limited by availability of resources. In order to update the current population estimate for the Southern Beaufort Sea, the USGS/BRD, the Service, and the Canadian Wildlife Service would conduct a five year intensive mark/recapture study in the Southern Beaufort Sea.

The need to develop a statistically valid population estimate for the Chukchi/Bering Seas population stock continues to be one of our greatest needs. Population information is essential to implement the United States-Russia Bilateral Polar Bear Agreement and develop management goals and objectives for this stock. (Note: Development of this Bilateral Agreement continued through 1999 and 2000. It was signed on October 16, 2000, by representatives from both countries.) In 2000, an aerial survey was conducted along the ice edge from the U.S.-Russian border to Barrow, Alaska, using helicopters from a USCG icebreaker. The objectives of this survey were to estimate polar bear density for the eastern Chukchi Sea area and evaluate the potential for assistance by the USCG for more extensive surveys in the Chukchi Sea, particularly in Russian territory.

Pacific Walrus

The Pacific walrus population is an ecologically important component of the Bering/Chukchi Sea ecosystem. While foraging for clams and other invertebrates, walrus exert a strong influence on the structure of the benthic community and play an important role in nutrient cycling. Walrus also serve as an important food source for top level predators, including man. Pacific walrus have been harvested by subsistence hunters for thousands of years. Today, walrus hunting remains an important component of the economy and culture of Native communities along the Bering Sea and Chukchi Sea coasts.

The Service is responsible for managing walrus in U.S. waters. Authority and structure for management activities come from the Act. The essential guidance of the Act is to maintain marine mammal stocks as healthy and vital components of the marine ecosystem. In 1994, the Service developed a conservation plan for Pacific walrus. The plan identifies critical management and research needs and objectives for improving the conservation of walrus stocks in Alaska. The Service has used this plan to develop and implement walrus program activities as reported below.

International Activities in 1999 and 2000
The Pacific walrus is thought to be represented by a single stock of animals that inhabits the Bering and Chukchi Seas. The population ranges across the international boundaries of the United States and Russia, and both Nations share common interests with respect to its conservation and management.

In 1999, we, the EWC, and the Alaska Department of Fish and Game (ADFG) sponsored a pilot walrus harvest monitoring project in Chukotka, Russia. The project was designed to collect walrus harvest information from the six primary walrus hunting villages in Chukotka utilizing a network of local Native harvest monitors. Russian collaborators in the project included Chukotka TNIRO, the Naukan Native Corporation, and the Eskimo Society of Chukotka.

In May 1999, Russian harvest monitors traveled to Gambell, Alaska, to observe and participate in U.S. walrus harvest monitoring training. At the training session, the harvest monitors were provided with data forms and field equipment necessary to carry out harvest monitoring activities in their villages. Between May and October 1999, a total of 891 walrus were recorded by Russian harvest monitors in the villages of New Chaplino, Siriniki, Enmelen, Lorino, Uelen, and Inchoun. Researchers from the two countries exchanged their respective harvest monitoring reports in 2000.

In 2000, we, along with the EWC and the National Park Service sponsored the second season of walrus harvest monitoring in Chukotka. The villages of New Chaplino, Siriniki, Enmelen, Yanrakinot, Lorino, Uelen, Inchoun, and Enurmino were monitored. During the year, we also collected information on the walrus harvest by Alaska Natives in the major Alaskan walrus hunting communities. Harvest monitors in both countries collected harvest data directly through observation and hunter interviews in the villages. Researchers from the two countries had planned to

exchange their respective walrus harvest monitoring reports in 2001.

The Service and the USGS/BRD also sponsored a walrus haulout monitoring program in the Gulf of Anadyr, Chukotka, Russia. Russian biologists staffed terrestrial haulout sites at Rudder and Meechkin Spits from June through September. The objective of the study was to evaluate the size and composition of walrus herds at these important summer haulout sites in Russia.

Co-Management Activities With Alaska Natives in 1999 and 2000
The 1994 amendments to the Act included provisions for funding co-management activities for marine mammal stocks through cooperative agreements between the Service and Alaska Native organizations. The Act's Section 119 authorized funds to be appropriated to the Secretary of Interior (up to $1 million) and the Secretary of Commerce (up to $1.5 million) to implement this Section. Congress appropriated $250,000 for the Secretary of Interior to carry out this section in Fiscal Years 1999 and 2000. Of this money in each of these years, the Alaska Nanuuq Commission (ANC) received $90,000, the EWC received $80,000, and TASSC received $70,000. A Cooperative Agreement between each Commission and the Service incorporates specific project plans outlining how the funds will be used.

Specific activities undertaken by the EWC as part of its Cooperative Agreement with the Service included: a bilateral walrus harvest monitoring workshop; meetings with Chukotka Natives for the development of a native-to-native agreement on walrus conservation; a walrus harvest monitoring project in Russia; initial discussion of development of native self-regulation policies concerning walrus utilization; and an internship program providing the opportunity for native students to participate in walrus management and research activities.

Subsistence Walrus Hunt on Round Island, Bristol Bay, Alaska
In 1995, the Service entered into a cooperative management agreement with the Qayassik Walrus Commission (QWC), the EWC, and the ADFG to monitor a limited subsistence hunt on Round Island, Walrus Islands State Game Sanctuary, Bristol Bay, Alaska. For both years, the Round Island subsistence hunt was monitored by the Bristol Bay Native Association (BBNA), with the Service providing technical support in the form of training,

equipment, and specimen analysis. The hunt monitor traveled to and from the island with the hunting crews. The harvest limit of 20 walrus for both years, including struck and lost animals, was divided by the QWC between eight Bristol Bay villages; and the harvest season each year was from September 20 to October 20.

In 1999, 13 walrus were harvested by hunters from six different villages. No animals were struck and lost. Whenever possible, lower canine teeth were collected and turned over to the Service for age determination. In 2000, eight walrus were harvested by hunters from three different villages. One animal was struck and lost. Copies of the Round Island walrus harvest monitoring report are available from the Service's Alaska Marine Mammals Management Office, 1011 East Tudor Road, Anchorage, Alaska 99503.

Research and Monitoring Activities in 1999 and 2000 - Bristol Bay Walrus Haulouts
Bristol Bay provides critical feeding and resting habitat for a large number of male Pacific walrus. From May through October, walrus congregate in the Bay and rest at terrestrial haulout sites at Round Island, Cape Peirce, Cape Newenham, and Cape Seniavin. Each summer, Service biologists monitor the number of walrus using the haulouts, and record and report any incidences of human-caused disturbances. Monitoring these haulouts provides a cost-effective source of information on trends in the number of male walrus utilizing the Bristol Bay region. Monitoring efforts are expected to provide information on haulout patterns and trends in local habitat use. These monitoring activities have contributed to specific regulations such as fishing closure zones to protect walrus at these critical sites.

In 1999, all four Bristol Bay haulouts were monitored by Service employees, interns, and volunteers. Round Island was monitored from May 17 through August 10. Monitors reported a high average count of 4,186 walrus on July 8. Cape Peirce was monitored from May 29 through October 8 with a reported high average count of 2,263 walrus on August 8. Cape Newenham was monitored from June 24 to July 20. A high count of three walrus was noted on July 10. Cape Seniavin was monitored from June 28 through July 20. Monitors reported a high average count of 1,556 on July 5.

The 1999 monitoring season marked the second year of the BBNA Youth Student Internship Program. This is a cooperative program between BBNA and the Service, in which an Alaska Native undergraduate participates in all phases of the field work at Cape Seniavin, data management, and report generation. The haulout at Cape Seniavin does not have the protection that the haulouts at Round Island and on the Togiak National Wildlife Refuge have. Haulout monitors at Cape Seniavin recorded 30 human-caused disturbances during the 25 day field season. One of the more severe disturbances was caused by a small plane passing north to south within 400m of the haulout at an altitude of approximately 180 feet. All walrus on the beach oriented to the noise and most of them (76 percent) abandoned the haulout.

In addition to monitoring haulouts from the ground, the Service collected aerial photographs of Round Island on several dates in July 1999. Analysis of those photographs indicate that when viewed from above, the average walrus covers 2.2 m2 of ground. This technique can be used to estimate the number of walrus on a haulout from remotely sensed data, including airborne and satellite imagery.

In the summer of 2000, haulouts at Round Island were monitored from May 6 through August 16. Our monitors reported a high count of 7,573 animals on 8 August. This was the highest peak count since 1995 when 9,550 animals were counted on Round Island. Haulouts at Cape Peirce were monitored from 26 April to 5 October. The peak count of walrus at Cape Peirce was 971 on June 23. This was the lowest peak count since haulout monitoring began at Cape Peirce in 1981. The previous low peak number was 1,474 in 1990.

Cape Newenham haulouts were monitored from 20 June to 19 July. The peak number of walrus hauled out at Cape Newenham this year was four animals on 1 July. The walrus haulout at Cape Seniavin was not monitored in 2000 due to logistical problems. The Service had planned to monitor all four Bristol Bay haulouts in 2001. Field reports for haulout monitoring activities in Bristol Bay are available from the U.S. Fish and Wildlife Service, Marine Mammals Management Office.

Walrus Harvest Monitoring Project
The Walrus Harvest Monitoring Project (WHMP) monitors the size and structure of the subsistence walrus harvest in the primary walrus hunting villages in Alaska. Service and village technicians work together to collect information on the size and demographics of the spring harvest by conducting hunter interviews and obtaining biological samples. This information is used to assess the size and composition of the harvest and to study aspects of walrus population dynamics and life history. Samples collected through the WHMP include teeth for age determination, adult female reproductive tracts to determine reproductive status, and occasional anomalous tissues which are used to identify specific pathologies.

In 1999, a total of 2,195 harvested Pacific walrus were recorded through the WHMP at the Native villages of Little Diomede, Gambell, Savoonga, and Wales. This was the largest harvest recorded by WHMP monitors in the past 15 years. The monitored harvest consisted of: 1,685 adults, 78 subadults, 19 yearlings, 408 calves, and 5 animals of unknown age class. Of the noncalf walrus taken where sex was identified, 1,312 (73.6 percent) were females and 471 (26.4 percent) were males, a 2.8:1 F:M ratio.

In early 2000, a study plan was approved to continue monitoring the spring walrus harvest in these four Native Alaskan villages and to expand this program into the village of Shishmaref. These five villages are currently responsible for approximately 65-90 percent of the reported annual Alaskan walrus harvest each year.

In 2000, a total of 1,615 harvested Pacific walrus were recorded through the WHMP at Little Diomede, Gambell, Savoonga, Wales, and Shishmaref. The monitored harvest consisted of: 1,195 adults, 35 subadults, 1 yearling, 381 calves, and 3 animals of unknown age class. Of the noncalf walrus taken where sex was identified, 823 (69.1 percent) were females and 368 (30.9 percent) were males, a 2.2:1 F:M ratio. The Service and the EWC will monitor the spring walrus harvest in these five villages in 2001. A field report of walrus harvest monitoring activities in Alaska is available from the U.S. Fish and Wildlife Service, Marine Mammals Management Office.

Population Status and Trend
The current size and trend of the Pacific walrus population are unknown. Cooperative aerial surveys by the United States and the Soviet Union (now Russia) were carried out at 5-year intervals between 1975 and 1990; however, population estimates generated from these surveys were considered imprecise and not useful for detecting population trends. Cooperative aerial surveys were suspended after 1990 due to unresolved problems with survey methods and lack of resources in the United States and Russia. Recent scientific observations and reports from Native hunters suggest that the rate of recruitment of calves into the population has been low for the past several years. It is unknown whether the walrus population has been affected by ecosystem changes that have contributed to declines in other species of marine mammals and sea birds in the Bering Sea. Future work to evaluate the size and trend of the Pacific walrus population is considered a high priority by both Russian and U.S. scientists.

The lack of precision and reliability in the fall surveys conducted in the past has prompted the Service to revisit the question of how best to monitor status and trends in walrus abundance. In March 2000, the Service and the USGS hosted a workshop on walrus survey

USFWS

Pacific walrus

methods. Workshop participants included U.S. and Russian experts in walrus biology and survey design, resource users, and managers. The goals of the workshop were to revisit the question of how best to obtain population estimates and track trends in walrus abundance. Questions concerning the best time, location, and techniques to survey walrus stocks were examined. Recommendations from the workshop centered on three primary issues: (1) ability to estimate a correction factor for the number of animals in the water as opposed to the number of animals visible on the ice; (2) applicability of remote sensing to improve accuracy of counts; and (3) potential for use of mark/recapture approach. Work is underway to address workshop recommendations, and studies are planned to test a different type of transmitter attachment and various remote sensing techniques. A project was initiated to develop a study design for a mark/recapture approach. Walrus can be individually identified based on genetic analysis, and the "marks" would be based on biopsy samples. A report summarizing the proceedings of the walrus census workshop is available from the U.S. Fish and Wildlife Service, Marine Mammals Management Office.

Walrus Productivity and Survivorship
Over the past few years there has been a growing body of evidence that changes in the walrus population are occurring. Many subsistence hunters throughout Alaska have reported that they are seeing fewer numbers of newborn calves in recent years. The traditional knowledge supplied by these hunters is consistent with recent reports from scientists who have been surveying the ice pack in the Chukchi Sea between Alaska and Russia to assess the age and sex composition of walrus herds. In 1999, shipboard surveys of the pack ice in the Chukchi and Bering Seas were used to visually sample the age-sex composition of free-ranging walrus herds in order to investigate productivity and juvenile survival rates. Preliminary results of the shipboard surveys indicate that the number of 1 year-old, 2 year-old, and 3 year-old calves per 100 adult females was lower than expected, suggesting that productivity and/or juvenile survival among Pacific walruses has been low for at least the past five years.

The cause of the suppressed productivity and/or juvenile survival rates is unknown, but warrants further investigation. The Service contacted the USCG Arctic Icebreaker Committee to express interest in performing ice-edge walrus surveys in 2001. Information on ice conditions and distribution of walrus herds may also be useful for planning future large-scale population surveys.

Northern Sea Otter
In 1999 and 2000, the Alaska sea otter program accomplished the activities described in detail below. Many constitute co-management activities and were conducted in close cooperation with TASSC under Section 119 of the Act. The Service and TASSC continue to work together under co-management on the development of regional and local management plans, collection, and use of traditional Native ecological knowledge, sharing of scientific information, and implementation of the biological monitoring program.

Co-management with Alaska Natives in 1999 and 2000

Biosampling Program
The Service continued to work with the TASSC on the ongoing training of Alaska Native hunters in sea otter necropsy techniques. A total of 56 individuals have been trained in communities throughout Alaska. This has resulted in the collection of sea otter biological samples for contaminants analyses and life history studies. Through 2000, a total of 344 sea otters that were taken through subsistence hunting have been necropsied as part of this program; 21 of that total was in 1999 while 26 sea otters were necropsied and sampled in 2000. In addition to collecting baseline information about sea otters in Alaska, this program has been the source of samples for ongoing studies on sea otter population structure and health.

Mortality Surveys
In several communities, annual sea otter carcass surveys are being conducted by local Native residents to assess winter mortality. The program involves volunteers searching specific beaches early in the spring, and collecting information on the carcasses of otters that have died during the previous winter. The communities of False Pass, Cordova, and Sitka have had ongoing survey programs, and the communities of Port Heiden and Unalaska started their programs this year. During early 1999, residents of Port Heiden were able to document the movement of sea otters across the Alaska Peninsula from Bristol Bay toward the Pacific Ocean, and mortality associated with that event. Local participation provides an opportunity to track this type of valuable information. In 2000, surveys were conducted in conjunction with Service personnel to document winter mortality in Cordova and Port Heiden.

Traditional Knowledge
An important information source is the traditional knowledge of residents throughout the Alaska Native communities. This historical information can then be incorporated into the management of sea otters. During 1999, the Sitka Marine Mammal Commission published a local knowledge survey on sea otter distribution in Southeast Alaska. A second effort was initiated in Southwest Alaska involving documentation of the observations of local residents regarding past and current interactions between killer whales and sea otters. The community of False Pass has started this survey in their community.

Killer Whale Photo Identification
In an effort to investigate killer whale predation on the sea otter population in the Aleutian Islands, training in photo identification methods of killer whale identification was initiated during 1999. The objective of this training was to have local residents help in the documentation of transient killer whales in areas of potential sea otter conflict. Although training efforts got off to a slow start due to the absence of killer whales, community involvement was beneficial in developing local participation for information exchanges.

Genetics Stock Identification
The Service began work during 1999 on a statewide assessment of the genetics of sea otters, in order to better define the stock structure of the population. This project will utilize the genetics samples collected through the Biosampling Program and is being conducted in cooperation with TASSC. The goal of this project is to supplement prior population genetics work done with mitochondrial DNA with analyses of several nuclear DNA markers (microsatellites) to define the stock structure of sea otters in Alaska. Inclusion of genetics samples collected through the sea otter Biosampling Program and our Marking, Tagging, and Reporting Program (MTRP) has increased the sample size to over 300 samples.

Sea Otter Population Trend Surveys
During 2000, local sea otter population trend surveys continued in the communities of Cordova, Port Graham/Nanwalek, Yakutat, Unalaska, and Sitka. Survey training was held in conjunction with USGS/BRD at Adak, Alaska. Training was also initiated at Whittier, Alaska.

TASSC and Tribal Projects
There were a number of activities involving TASSC and tribal projects in 2000. Co-management funds supported various participation by TASSC representatives in local, Federal, and international meetings and workshops.

For example, efforts were made to initiate co-management activities in Southeast Alaska (Prince of Wales Island) through tribal meetings. In addition, TASSC members participated in a British Columbia Sea Otter Workshop, Marine Mammal Protection Act reauthorization hearings, and the seventh United States-Russia Area V Sea Otter Workshop in Monterey, California. In an effort to facilitate resource information from the Alaska Peninsula and Kodiak Island, TASSC representatives attended the Bristol Bay Marine Mammal Council meeting and participated in drafting the South Alaska Peninsula Sea Otter Regional Management Plan. TASSC and tribal representatives also participated in varying degrees during the Aleutian sea otter aerial survey.

Research and Monitoring Activities in 1999 and 2000

Contaminants Monitoring

A 3-year program was initiated in 1997 to monitor contaminants in approximately 50 sea otters. Funding was received from the Service's Division of Environmental Contaminants to analyze livers and kidneys from 56 sea otters harvested by Alaska Natives throughout the State. Samples were submitted for organochlorine and heavy metal analyses from southeast Alaska (20 otters), Prince William Sound (17 otters), Kodiak Archipelago (7 otters), Cook Inlet (6 otters), the Alaska Peninsula/Aleutian Islands (4 otters), and the Russian Kamchatka Peninsula (2 otters).

Initial results indicate that the levels of most pollutants were below or near detection levels. The Service is in the process of reviewing laboratory results relative to quality assurance criteria and completing statistical analyses of all data. Results were summarized in a draft interim technical report in June 2000. This report was finalized in 2001.

Sea Otter Population Survey in Izembek Lagoon

The Marine Mammals Management Office collaborated with the Izembek National Wildlife Refuge in the summer of 1999 to conduct an aerial survey of sea otter abundance in Izembek Lagoon. Historically, large numbers of sea otters have inhabited that lagoon with some seasonal variation depending on sea ice coverage. This was a first step in assessing potential changes in sea otter abundance on the north Aleutian basin and to examine another lagoon that may serve as a refuge for sea otters from predation by killer whales.

Work with the USGS/BRD Alaska Science Center, Population Surveys

Information collected in the mid-1990s by the USGS/BRD at several locations in the western and central Aleutian Islands indicated a dramatic decline in the sea otter population over the past decade. In order to determine the magnitude and geographic extent of the decline, in April 2000, the Service repeated an aerial survey of the entire Aleutian archipelago for comparison with data collected in 1992. The results of this survey indicate an overall population decline of 70 percent over the past eight years. Analysis of both aerial and skiff survey data from select islands corroborate both the timing and magnitude of the decline.

On August 22, 2000, the Director of the Service designated sea otters in the Aleutian Islands as a candidate species under the ESA. The Service requested funds for Federal Fiscal Year 2001 to prepare a proposed rule to list the sea otter; however, due to other priorities, those funds were not available. The Service also received a petition to list the sea otter. Having already been elevated to candidate species status, this petition was treated as a second, redundant petition.

Immediately following the Aleutian survey, the Service conducted another aerial survey of sea otters along the north side of the Alaska Peninsula.

This area contains a broad, shallow shelf extending over 20 miles from shore and was last surveyed in 1986. In order to document the eastward extent of the Aleutian decline, the Service replicated that survey design in May 2000. Results from this survey indicate that sea otters have also declined by as much as 36-56 percent along the north side of the Alaska Peninsula. The Service surveyed the south side of the Peninsula in 2001.

During both years, the Service continued to work with the USGS/BRD to identify sea otter research needs and provide management information on various issues. In response to unusually high winter mortality in the Cordova area, the Service in 2000 funded USGS/BRD to conduct an aerial survey of Orca Inlet in Prince William Sound. The estimate from this survey effort was 3,455 sea otters. It did not appear that large numbers of sea otters were moving into or out of Orca Inlet on a short term basis (Bodkin, personal communication).

Genetics Studies

In November, 2000, the Service completed the analysis portion of a statewide sea otter genetics study. Conducted in cooperation with TASSC, this study utilized genetics samples collected through the Marine Mammal Marking, Tagging, and Reporting Program and the Sea Otter Biosampling Program. This project supplemented earlier population genetics work based on mitochondrial DNA with analyses of several nuclear DNA microsatellites to define the stock structure of sea otters in Alaska. Data from two of the microsatellites tested were acceptable and thus used for regional comparison. The results were consistent with a previous mitochondrial DNA studies and therefore support the identification of multiple sea otter stocks in Alaska.

Douglas Burn/USFWS

Rescued northern sea otter pup

Polar Bear

International Activities in 1999 and 2000-U.S./Russia Bilateral Agreement In February 1998, United States and Russian representatives negotiated a preliminary text for the United States-Russia Bilateral Agreement on the Conservation and Management of the Chukchi/Bering Seas Polar Bear Population. In July 1999, comments received from the Russian government indicated substantial changes.

Additional discussions between the two sides ensued and a meeting took place in March 2000 to finalize the Agreement. In Washington, D.C., on October 16, 2000, the Assistant Secretary of State for the United States and the Russian Ambassador to the United States signed the landmark bilateral conservation agreement entitled, Agreement between the United States of America and the Russian Federation on the Conservation and Management of the Alaska-Chukotka Polar Bear Population.

This Agreement significantly advances on-the-ground conservation programs for this shared population of polar bears. The purpose of the Bilateral Agreement is to provide for effective conservation and management of the polar bear population in the Chukchi/Bering Seas through regulation of take and protection of habitat. The Bilateral Agreement would provide the basis for developing a unified and comprehensive management program which includes provisions for regulation of take (enforceable quotas), enhanced biomonitoring and research opportunities, habitat protection, and nonconsumptive as well as consumptive uses. It provides the mechanism to regulate the harvest prior to depletion. The treaty between governments would be implemented through cooperative management arrangements with Alaska and Chukotka Natives. A joint Commission consisting of a Government and a Native representative from each country will design the management programs, describe how these programs will be carried out, and provide oversight for implementation of the Agreement.

Future steps include advice and consent to ratification by the Senate and advancing companion draft legislation and interpretive documents to Congress.

Co-Management with Alaska Natives in 1999 and 2000
The ANC was established on June 16, 1994, to represent Alaska Native hunters concerning issues related to the conservation and subsistence uses of polar bears. The ANC consists of representatives from 15 villages from northern and western coastal Alaska.

The goals of the ANC are to: (1) encourage and implement self-regulation of polar bear hunting by Alaska Natives; (2) provide education and information to the public, State, and Federal agencies; (3) represent polar bear hunting communities in developing, reviewing, and commenting on regulations affecting polar bear management; (4) encourage international cooperation in management, research, and enforcement through the involvement of Native hunters and leaders to ensure the health of polar bears and their habitat; (5) promote conservation, health, and sustainable utilization of polar bears by Alaska Natives; (6) actively participate in the formation and implementation of harvest monitoring efforts; and (7) enter into or participate in the negotiation of local, State, Federal, and international agreements for the protection, enforcement, enhancement, utilization,

and research of polar bears and other marine mammal populations.

In 1999, $90,000 was provided to the ANC by the Service, as authorized under Section 119 of the Act. These funds were used for activities associated with the development of the Native-to-Native Agreement for the conservation of polar bears in the Chukchi/Bering Seas and participation in international, Federal, and local meetings to support Native interests in polar bear conservation and to assist in the development of the United States/Russia Bilateral Agreement. In addition, the ANC participated in meetings in Gambell and Savoonga, both of which are on St. Lawrence Island, Alaska, to discuss the implications of the U.S./Russia Bilateral Agreement and to provide information concerning the health, management, subsistence use, and conservation of polar bears to local subsistence users.

The ANC is also conducting a National Park Service funded study to collect traditional knowledge of polar bear habitat use in Chukotka, Russia. The Service is providing technical assistance to facilitate completion of this project, which is similar to a study previously conducted in Alaska.

Again in 2000, $90,000 was provided by the Service to the ANC. Specific accomplishments for 2000 include: (1) four meetings with the Indigenous Peoples Council on Marine Mammals (IPCoMM) to discuss reauthorization of the MMPA; (2) continued work on development of the Native-to-Native Agreement for the conservation of polar bears in the Chukchi/Bering Seas; (3) initial preparations for meetings in each village to discuss implementation of the United States/Russia Bilateral Agreement and the Native-to-Native Agreement; and (4) development and distribution of posters on co-management to all the village councils and several schools.

The Inuvialuit Game Council and North Slope Borough meeting of Joint Commissioners and Technical Advisors was held March 3-4, 2000, in Inuvik, Northwest Territories, Canada. This meeting is held primarily to review the status and effectiveness of the 1988 Inuvialuit Game Council/North Slope Borough Polar Bear Agreement (IGC/NSB Agreement). The IGC/NSB Agreement is a Native-to-Native Agreement that sets guidelines for management of the Southern Beaufort Sea polar bear population that is shared between the United States and Canada. The Service, which participates as a technical advisor to the commission,

prepared a report that summarized the harvest, management, and research activities for this population in the past year. A manuscript evaluating the effects of the first 10 years of the IGC/NSB Agreement is in preparation.

The NSB discontinued its highly effective polar bear patrols in 2000 due to budget constraints. The Service and the NSB are developing a Polar Bear/Human Conflict Plan, and strategy to fund implementation of this Plan.

Future ANC tasks are to: (1) finalize the Native-to-Native Polar Bear Agreement with the Chukotka Union of Marine Mammal Hunters (UMMH); (2) conduct meetings in Alaska villages to discuss implementation of the United States-Russia Bilateral Agreement; (3) assist the Service in collecting harvest data and specimens; (4) develop a long range strategic plan for the ANC; and (5) support and encourage conservation and wise use of polar bears.

Research and Monitoring in 1999 and 2000

Harvest Summary
Our MTRP continued to collect information from polar bears taken by Alaska Native hunters for subsistence purposes during the past year. In addition to the 92 bears tagged by the MTRP during harvest year 1998/99, we received information of an additional 9 bears harvested but not yet tagged. The majority of the harvest (79 percent) was from the Chukchi/Bering Seas region in western Alaska.

Polar bears were harvested in every month of the year. These predators typically follow the ice edge and thus are not available to hunters in western Alaska until after January, when the pack ice reaches this area. A majority (81 percent) of the bears were killed during late winter and early spring (January-May). The fall (i.e., September, October, and November) harvest was below the historical average.

We obtained premolar teeth for age determination from 75 of the 101 bears harvested during the 1998/99 season. These teeth were analyzed in 2000, and the following age determinations were made. The mean age of females (4.9 years, n=28) and males (5.5 years, n=47) were below the long term average of 7.1 and 6.5, respectively.

During harvest year 1999/2000, the Service again collected information from polar bears harvested by Native hunters. Only 45 polar bears were reported through the MTRP. Information was also gathered from 15 polar bears that were not reported. The sex composition of the reported and unreported harvest of 59 bears was 41 males, 9 females, and 9 unknown. Approximately half of the harvest (32/59) came from the Chukchi/Bering Seas population in western Alaska.

Polar bears were harvested in every month except June and October. Hunters in western Alaska, from Point Lay to St Lawrence Island, typically harvest bears after December. This is the result of bears moving southward with the advancing pack ice. Thus they are not available in this area until later in the season. Since 1980, significantly more bears have been harvested in the fall (October-December) in the Southern Beaufort Sea than in the Chukchi Sea. The sex ratio of known-sex bears harvested during 1999/2000 was 82 percent males and 18 percent females.

The Service obtained premolar teeth for age determination from 20 of the bears harvested during the 1999/2000 season. Results from these teeth, sent in for age determination, currently are not available.

Polar Bear Management Agreement, Beaufort Sea

The IGC/NSB Agreement sets recommended harvest guidelines for the Southern Beaufort Sea stock of polar bears. The 1998/99 harvest for the participating North Slope villages was 14 polar bears, which was roughly 15 percent of the statewide total. Bears were harvested in all months except December. Seven bears were taken outside the prescribed season which extends from September 1 to May 31.

The sex composition of known-sex animals was 53 percent (8/15) male and 47 percent (7/15) female. The proportion of females in the harvest exceeded the 33 percent recommended in the IGC/NSB Agreement, which sets the sustainable yield based on a 2:1 male:female ratio in the harvest. Based on information from the last 15 years, the average age of the harvest has remained relatively constant with a proportion of bears reaching old age. The age class composition from the 1997/98 harvest was 47 percent adults, 35 percent subadults, and 18 percent cubs and approximated the long-term average, since the inception of the IGC/NSB Agreement in 1988.

The 1999/2000 harvest for villages of the North Slope, party to the IGC/NSB Agreement was 22 polar bears. This harvest was well below the 40 bear sustainable harvest quota, the recommended harvest guidelines for the Southern Beaufort Sea population, set by the IGC/NSB Agreement. Bears were harvested in all months except June, October, and March. Two bears were taken outside the September 1 to May 31 recommended season.

The sex composition of the harvest was 20 males and 2 females. This represents the lowest proportion of females in the harvest since the inception of the IGC/NSB Agreement and is well below the recommended harvest guidelines of 33 percent. Although complete sex information provided by the hunter and/or tagger was available for 24 of 27 bears in the 1999/2000 harvest, teeth were collected from only seven bears.

Polar Bear Biomonitoring Program

The fourth year of the polar bear biomonitoring program, which coincides with the polar bear harvest period, began in fall/winter 1998-1999. As in previous years, Service biologists visited Native villages in northern and western Alaska to review the biological sampling protocol with polar bear hunters and MTRP taggers, encourage participation in the contaminant sampling program, assist in the collection, and explain the need and rationale for collecting polar bear samples. Regular contact with key residents assisting in the specimen collection is ongoing.

To date, organochlorine analyses has been completed for 24 adult males, eight from the Beaufort Sea population and 16 from the Chukchi/Bering Seas population. Levels of total polychlorinated biphenyls (S-PCBs ppm wet weight) averaged 2.41 ppm (n=24, range 0.90-5.06 ppm), which is below levels recorded in Hudson Bay, Canada, and Svalbard, Norway, two areas which have some of the highest documented levels of PCBs in polar bears. The highest levels of S-PCB were found in the one subadult from Point Lay (7.55 ppm) and three adult males from Barrow and Savoonga (5.06 ppm, 5.01 ppm, and 5.05 ppm). Six congeners 99, 153, 138, 180, 170, and 194 constituted approximately 87 percent of the S-PCB in the sample.

Mean levels of total hexachlorocyclo-hexane (S-HCH ppm wet weight) for the 24 bears recently analyzed was 0.87 which is similar to the high levels reported for the Chukchi and Bering Seas by Norstrom et al. (19981). Beta-HCH, the most persistent HCH isomer, constituted about 92 percent of the sum HCHs. The levels of S-HCH in the Chukchi/Bering Seas and Beaufort Sea polar bears are among the highest reported within the Arctic region. Suspected sources are from Asia, carried north via the Japanese current, and from Russian rivers to the north.

Nineteen trace elements were analyzed in the muscle, livers, and kidneys of 22 adult male polar bears taken in northern and western Alaska. Only 14 samples were used to calculate the average methyl mercury levels because some of the mercury levels in the muscle samples were below the detection limit. The methyl mercury/mercury ratios in the muscle tissues averaged 37 percent. Several elements (i.e., aluminum-Al, arsenic-As, boron-B, barium-Ba, beryllium-Be, molybdenum-Mo, lead-Pb) were near the detection limit in all tissues. The preliminary results (n=21) indicate that mercury (Hg) levels in Alaska polar bear livers (both population stocks combined) are lower than those reported for western Canada in 1986 and levels of cadmium (Cd) and Copper (Cu) are somewhat higher.

Polar bear feeding

[1]Norstrom, R.J., S.E. Belikov, E.W. Born, G.W. Garner, B. Malone, S. Olpinski, M.A. Ramsay, S. Schliebe, I. Sterling, M.S. Stishov, M.K. Taylor, and O. Wiig. 1998. Chlorinated hydrocarbon contaminants in polar bears from eastern Russia, North America, Greenland, and Svalbard: Biomonitoring of Arctic pollution. Archives of Environmental Contamination and Toxicology 35: 354-367.

Population Monitoring
The Act requires the Service to manage polar bear populations at the optimum sustainable population (OSP) level. Although population estimates are available for the Southern Beaufort Sea population in northern Alaska, these estimates are becoming dated. A simultaneous sampling effort in Canada and Alaska will be required to develop a more reliable population estimate for the Southern Beaufort Sea.

Population data is limited for the Chukchi/Bering Seas population in western Alaska. Consequently, OSP and PBR levels currently cannot be determined for the Chukchi/Bering Seas population and accurate population information is needed.

In August, we conducted a pilot study from a U.S. Coast Guard (USCG) Ship of Opportunity. The purposes of the study were to assess the reliability and logistical constraints of using helicopter support, to determine the feasibility of conducting future surveys in the Chukchi Sea from this platform, and to develop a baseline population density estimate. We flew line transect surveys from the USCG Cutter Polar Star using two Delphine H-65 helicopters. The survey efforts were conducted in the eastern Chukchi Sea and western Beaufort Sea.

We flew 8,734 km of randomly selected transect lines during 71 hours of survey effort on 43 flights. Surveys occurred between August 5, 2000, and August 28, 2000. Twenty-five groups consisting of 27 polar bears were seen on transect. Density estimates, based on preliminary analysis, ranged from .0060 bears/km2 (or 1 bear/168 km5) to .0065 bears/km2 (or 1 bear/154 km5).

Use of an icebreaker with helicopter support for future surveys holds promise. For statistically defensible population estimates to be developed, however, the sample size (number of bear groups observed on transect) must be increased and survey-specific correction factors developed for polar bears missed by observers.

Oil and Gas Polar Bear Surveys
The Beaufort Sea Northstar Project includes construction of the first offshore oil production facility incorporating subsea pipeline technology in Arctic North America. In February 1999, the U.S. Army Engineer District, Alaska, completed the Final Environmental Impact Statement, Beaufort Sea Oil and Gas Development/Northstar Project (Northstar EIS). The Northstar EIS identified potential effects of development and production of the Northstar Unit on the surrounding environment, and included stipulations to mitigate for potential effects. Stipulations require resource surveys to be conducted for sensitive species or habitats, including polar bears.

We conducted aerial surveys along the coastline and barrier islands of the Beaufort Sea in cooperation with BP Exploration and LGL Research from September 21, 2000, to October 12, 2000. We designed the aerial surveys to determine the spatial and temporal distribution and abundance of polar bears using coastal habitats and barrier islands during the open water period (until freeze-up) in the vicinity of offshore oil and gas operations. We made 232 observations of polar bears on four weekly surveys (49, 73, 72, and 38, respectively); some of the bears may have been observed on more than one survey. Barrier Islands represented the most used habitat (72 percent) followed by coastal mainland (17 percent), shore ice (9 percent), and open water (2 percent). Adult females and dependent young comprised 53 percent of the observations.

Incidental, Small Take During Oil and Gas Operations
In 1981 the Act was amended to allow for the incidental, but not intentional, take of small numbers of marine mammals during specific activities at specific geographic sites. Regulations to authorize and govern the incidental take of small numbers of polar bear and Pacific walrus during oil and gas industry operations (i.e., exploration, development, and production) in the southern Beaufort Sea and adjacent northern coast of Alaska expired January 28, 1999, at which time they were revised and issued through January 30, 2000, to allow information on the potential impact of subsea pipelines from the proposed Northstar project to become final. On December 9, 1999, a proposal to issue regulations for 3 years was published in the FEDERAL REGISTER. On March 30, 2000, after evaluating oil and gas activities including the offshore development at Northstar, we issued new regulations effective through March 31, 2003 (62 FR 16828).

During 1999, 35 Letters of Authorization (LOAs) were issued to the oil and gas industry under our Incidental Take Regulations. During 2000, we issued 62 LOAs (Table 1). Both years represent substantial increases in the number of oil and gas activities on the North Slope of Alaska from 1998 (20) and previous years (1990-1997, range 5-12).

Table 1. Letters of Authorization (LOA) issued in 2000 for the Beaufort Sea and adjacent northern coast of Alaska

Company	Exploration	Development	Production
PHILLIPS Alaska, Inc.	19		2
ARCO Alaska, Inc.	16	1	
Western Geophysical	10		
BP Exploration (Alaska), Inc.	4	3	2
Fairweather E&P Service, Inc.	3		
Exxon/Mobil Production Company	1	1	
Total	53	5	4

(Note: An additional offshore production site is in the review process. The Liberty Project has not been evaluated under existing incidental take regulations. To more accurately characterize potential environmental impacts to polar bears and their habitat from oil spills in the marine environment, polar bear population distribution modeling, and oil spill trajectory analysis are continuing. The Service, USGS/BRD, the Minerals Management Service (MMS), and the oil and gas industry are involved in this process. In addition, a large scale, two year National Research Council study of the cumulative effects of oil and gas development in Arctic Alaska is ongoing).

Marking, Tagging, and Reporting Program

Success of our MTRP, first implemented in October 1988 to monitor the subsistence harvest of polar bear, sea otter, and Pacific walrus, depends upon routine contact between the Service and the individuals hired in villages to do the actual tagging (i.e., taggers). During 1999, the MTRP staff traveled to 60 coastal villages to hold village meetings, hire and replace taggers, provide training, and work with hunters to gain better compliance with the MTRP regulations; in 2000, we made 53 such visits. To help inform village residents of these provisions, 15 school presentations were made during the village visits in 1999, while 11 schools were visited in 2000. In the Anchorage area, the MTRP staff conducted 14 other information and education programs in 1999 and 25 in 2000. During the two year period, the MTRP staff hired or replaced five taggers in 1999, and eight taggers in 2000.

In 1999, the MTRP had 147 taggers and 30 alternates located in 104 villages through coastal Alaska. In 2000, the number of taggers increased to 153 in the MTRP, along with 30 alternates located in 106 villages (Table 1, Map 1). Usually, local Native residents are hired and trained to work in villages where they live to tag polar bear and sea otter hides and skulls, and walrus tusks. The MTRP employed 66 sea otter, 25 polar bear, and 99 walrus taggers. The number of taggers per village varies depending on the magnitude of the harvest. Some villages have several taggers for each species and a few village taggers tag more than one species where the harvest numbers are low. Numbered, color coded, locking tags are placed on all polar bear and sea otter skulls and skins presented for tagging. Premolar teeth are extracted for aging purposes from each bear and otter skull. A lead headed wire tag is attached through a hole drilled in the root section of each walrus tusk tagged (beginning in 2001, plastic tags will be used). Tag numbers, location and date of tagging, place of kill or find, sex, age, and measurements of specified parts are recorded by the tagger. Harvest data were reported from 47 villages during 1999, and 66 villages during 2000.

Thirty-eight walrus taggers reported tagging 1,936 walrus in 1999, and 1,952 animals in 2000. Walrus tusks sometimes become separated before they are tagged. In order to accurately account for the harvest, a weight factor variable is added that interprets each record in terms of take. Estimation of the total harvest is made by summing this weight factor. Walrus records where only a single tusk was tagged is given a weight factor of 0.5, because the possibility exists that the second tusk may be tagged at a later date. For analytical purposes, the lower estimate is calculated with the assumption that single tusk-records in the database represent half of one walrus. The upper estimate is calculated assuming that each record represents a whole walrus. If all walrus tusks are tagged as pairs, the upper and lower bounds are equal. As a conservative approach to management, the upper estimate is considered to be the actual figure for the walrus harvest (Tables 6, 7).

Hunter success in both years varied greatly from village to village and between hunters. Many hunters reported poor weather and marginal ice conditions during the walrus migration making hunting conditions difficult. Often the villagers could hear or even see the walrus but because of bad ice conditions they were unable to get close to them.

Compliance with the tagging regulation by walrus hunters continues to need improvement. Despite an aggressive campaign by the MTRP staff and Law Enforcement, some walrus hunters still do not comply with the tagging rule. Village meetings, radio and newspaper announcements, letters, and posters were utilized to encourage the hunters in all villages to have every kill recorded. The most common reason for ivory not being tagged was that hunters carve their own harvested ivory. Some hunters do not see the use of tagging their ivory if they are going to use it themselves. In the past, when raw ivory was sold to the village store or registered agents, compliance with the rule was high.

Assessment of compliance is subjectively based on personal observation and discussions with village taggers and others. Enforcement of the tagging rule has been limited to only a few cases and those were related to other enforcement actions. However, information from the MTRP database was valuable in several enforcement actions in past years. In most cases, enforcement has had a positive effect and heightened awareness.

The MTRP staff maintained a village presence and routine contacts with taggers. They continued to hold village meetings, train and retrain taggers as necessary, work with native leaders and organizations and expand the use of informational and educational materials that relate to the MTRP and other marine mammal issues.

Because of the extensive exposure of the MTRP staff throughout coastal Alaska, MTRP personnel are often called upon by other programs in the Service that need an introduction to, or assistance working in, a village. The MTRP staff continued to provide information that is obtainable only by being acquainted with the residents of the remote villages and/or familiarity with the traditional village life.

During the two year period, we distributed our quarterly Marine Mammal Bulletin to all taggers and other interested people. The bulletin has proven to be valuable tool in disseminating pertinent information in a timely manner to a State-wide village audience.

Table 1. Villages With MTRP Taggers and Species Tagged.

Village	Species*	Village	Species*	Village	Species*
Adak	SO	Hydaburg	SO	Petersburg	SO
Akhiok	SO	Ivanof Bay	SO	Pilot Point	SO/W
Akutan	SO	Juneau	SO	Platinum	W
Aleknagik	W	Kake	SO	Point Hope	PB/W
Anchorage	SO/PB/W	Kaktovik	PB/W	Point Lay	PB/W
Angoon	SO	Karluk	SO	Port Graham	SO
Atka	SO	Kenai	SO/W	Port Heiden	SO/W
Barrow	PB/W	Ketchkan	SO	Port Lions	SO
Bethel	SO/W	King Cove	SO	Quinhagak	W
Brevig Mission	W	King Island	W	Sand Point	SO/W
Buckland	W	King Salmon	SO/W	Savoonga	PB/W
Chefornak	W	Kipnuk	W	Seldovia	SO
Chenega Bay	SO	Kivalina	PB/W	Shaktoolik	W
Chevak	W	Klawock	SO	Seward	SO
Chignik	SO/W	Kodiak	SO/W	Shishmaref	PB/W
Chignik Lagoon	SO	Kongiganak	W	Sitka	SO/W
Chignik Lake	SO/W	Kotzebue	PB/W	St. George	W
Clarks Point	W	Koyuk	W	St. Michael	W
Cold Bay	SO/W	Kwigillingok	W	St. Paul	SO/W
Cordova	SO/W	Larsen Bay	SO	Stebbins	W
Craig	SO	Little Diomede	PB/W	Tatitlek	SO
Deering	W	Manokotak	W	Teller	PB/W
Dillingham	SO/W	Mekoryuk	W	Togiak	W
Egegik	SO/W	Naknek	W	Toksook Bay	W
Elim	W	Nelson Lagoon	SO	Tuntutuliak	W
Emmonak	W	New Stuyahok	W	Tununak	W
English Bay	SO	Newtok	W	Twin Hills	W
Fairbanks	SO/PB/W	Nightmute	W	Unalakleet	W
False Pass	SO	Nikolski	SO	Unalaska	SO/W
Gambell	PB/W	Nome	PB/W	Valdez	SO
Golovin	W	Nuiqsut	PB	Wainwright	PB/W
Goodnews Bay	W	Old Harbor	SO	Wales	PB/W
Homer	SO/W	Ouzinkie	SO	Wrangell	SO
Hoonah	SO	Pelican	SO	Yakutat	SO
Hooper Bay	W	Perryville	SO/W		

*Species: SO = Sea Otter PB = Polar Bear W = Walrus

For names, addresses, and telephone numbers of village taggers, contact the U.S. Fish and Wildlife Service; Marine Mammals Management; Marking, Tagging, and Reporting Program; 1011 East Tudor Road; Anchorage, Alaska 99503, (800) 362-5148.

Map 1. Village locations with Marking, Tagging and Reporting Program taggers.

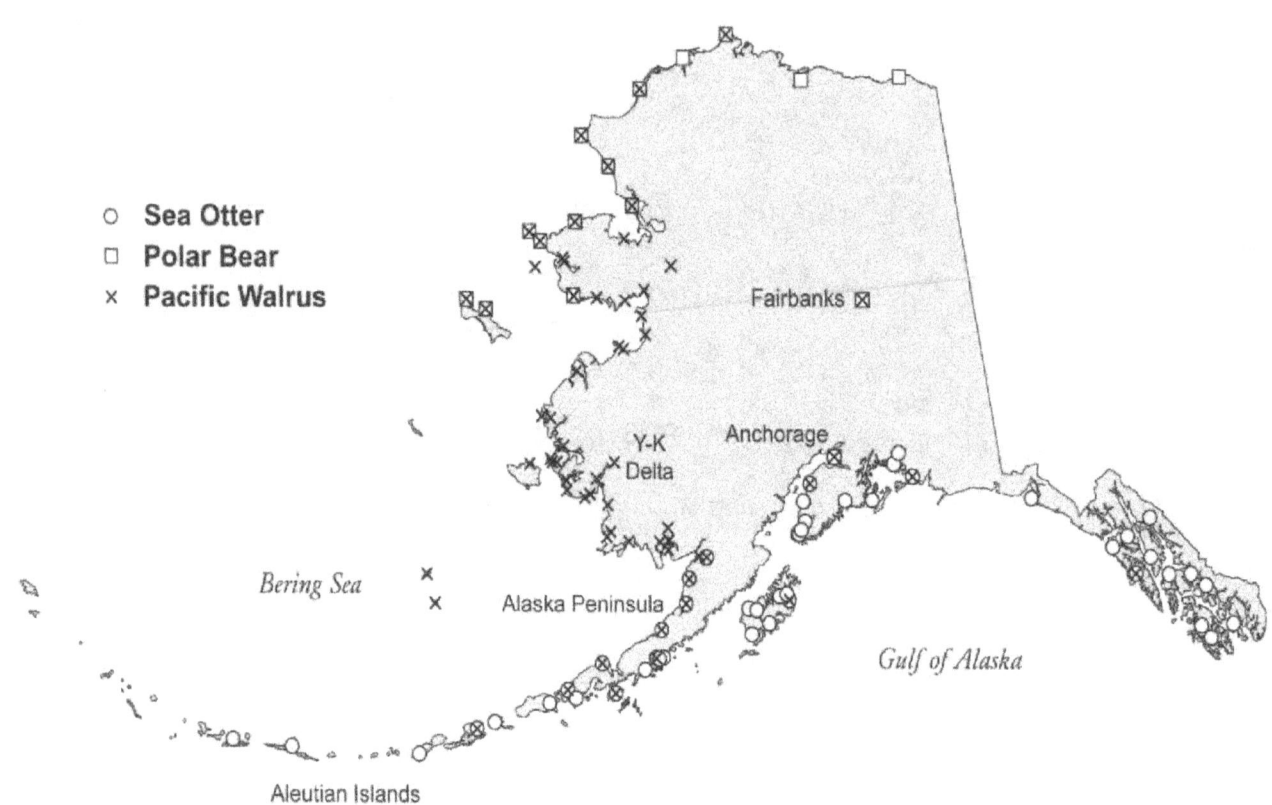

○ **Sea Otter**
□ **Polar Bear**
× **Pacific Walrus**

Fairbanks

Y-K
Delta

Anchorage

Bering Sea

Alaska Peninsula

Gulf of Alaska

Aleutian Islands

Twenty-nine sea otter taggers reported 531 otters being tagged in 1999, while 24 taggers reported 740 otters tagged in 2000 (Tables 2 and 3). Sea otter hides are used to make hats, gloves, slippers, blankets, and other arts and crafts. A few hunters trade sea otter hides for walrus ivory, polar bear and seal skins or other items that are used in making crafts. Compliance to the tagging regulation by sea otter hunters appears high.

Table 2. Sea otters tagged, by tagging location and year.

Location	Pre-Rule	1988-95	1996	1997	1998	1999	2000	Total
Adak	0	2	0	0	0	0	5	7
Akhiok	1	0	0	0	0	0	0	1
Akutan	0	11	0	0	0	0	0	11
Anchorage	117	192	50	22	2	50	21	454
Angoon	0	99	0	0	0	0	0	99
Atka	0	2	0	0	0	0	0	2
Bethel	4	1	0	0	0	0	0	5
Chenega Bay	0	14	6	13	0	5	10	48
Chignik	1	20	0	0	0	0	0	21
Chignik Lake	0	2	0	0	0	0	0	2
Cold Bay	0	9	0	0	0	0	1	10
Cordova	31	409	173	34	293	79	213	1,232
Craig	0	0	0	0	36	80	11	127
Egegik	0	0	1	0	0	0	0	1
English Bay	0	23	13	0	3	0	0	39
Fairbanks	0	2	0	0	0	0	0	2
False Pass	0	10	3	3	2	0	0	18
Homer	18	79	24	8	7	0	5	141
Hoonah	0	292	0	3	25	7	8	335
Hydaburg	0	0	7	38	1	31	95	172
Juneau	11	182	3	33	16	3	2	250
Kake	0	23	5	0	0	0	0	28
Kenai	0	66	0	0	2	0	0	68
Ketchikan	2	294	3	33	46	86	15	479
King Cove	8	40	0	13	1	2	5	69
King Salmon	0	1	0	0	0	1	0	2
Klawock	57	500	25	99	40	13	38	772
Kodiak	157	235	41	39	20	45	33	570
Larsen Bay	31	56	77	22	15	0	6	207
Mekoryuk	5	0	0	0	0	0	0	5
Nelson Lagoon	0	0	0	1	1	1	0	3
Nikolski	0	0	0	1	0	0	0	1
Old Harbor	0	0	0	53	0	0	0	53
Ouzinkie	0	29	0	0	0	0	0	29
Pelican	0	0	8	6	52	27	0	93
Perryville	0	4	0	0	0	0	0	4
Petersburg	0	0	0	10	0	0	0	10
Pilot Point	1	1	0	0	0	0	0	2
Port Graham	0	149	13	20	10	4	3	199
Port Heiden	1	9	7	1	1	4	4	27

Table 2. (cont.) Sea otters tagged, by tagging location and year.

Location	Pre-Rule	1988-95	1996	1997	1998	1999	2000	Total
Port Lions	11	27	18	9	5	3	1	74
Sand Point	0	17	0	4	2	8	0	31
Seldovia	0	41	1	27	11	0	0	80
Shishmaref	0	0	0	0	14	3	3	20
Sitka	44	696	71	97	113	69	146	1,236
Tatitlek	0	50	0	0	0	9	16	75
Unalaska	0	5	0	0	0	0	0	5
Valdez	0	431	56	167	111	78	69	912
Wrangell	0	23	3	0	0	1	6	33
Yakutat	0	42	4	13	31	1	24	115
Totals	500	4,088	612	769	860	610	740	8,179

Revised April 2, 2001

Table 3. Sea otters tagged by age, class, sex, and year.

Age	Sex	Pre-Rule	1988-95	1996	1997	1998	1999	2000	Total
A	F	88	972	82	96	106	105	172	1,621
A	M	231	2,362	422	488	611	348	434	4,896
A	U	121	207	42	62	37	74	25	568
P	F	0	14	5	4	7	2	5	37
P	M	1	28	5	11	6	10	6	67
P	U	6	16	2	4	1	2	1	32
S	F	8	140	20	45	46	32	34	325
S	M	8	236	31	48	40	36	59	458
S	U	14	41	3	11	6	1	4	80
U	F	0	9	0	0	0	0	0	9
U	M	0	4	0	0	0	0	0	4
U	U	23	59	0	0	0	0	0	82
Totals		500	4,088	612	769	860	610	740	8,179

Age Classes: A = Adult, S = Subadult, P = Pup, U = Unknown
Sex Classes: M = Male, F = Female, U = Unknown
Revised April 2, 2001

Ninety-two polar bears were tagged in 12 villages during the 1998/99 hunting season, with another 45 bears tagged in 11 villages during the 1999/00 season (Tables 4 and 5).

Table 4. Polar bears tagged, by tagging location and harvest year[a].

Village	1987/88-1994/95	1995/1996	1996/97	1997/98	1998/99	1999/00	Totals
Anchorage	13	0	0	0	0	0	13
Barrow	157	16	29	15	10	13	240
Brevig Mission	1	0	0	0	0	0	1
Fairbanks	1	0	0	0	0	0	1
Gambell	104	0	7	1	20	4	136
Kaktovik	23	1	2	1	1	1	29
Kivalina	20	0	0	0	3	0	23
Kotzebue	6	1	1	0	4	0	12
Little Diomede	63	2	6	3	4	5	83
Nome	6	0	0	1	0	0	7
Nuiqsut	9	1	0	2	2	5	19
Point Hope	98	3	13	10	15	6	145
Point Lay	10	0	5	3	0	2	20
Savoonga	86	0	1	5	11	4	107
Shishmaref	86	2	0	3	15	1	107
Wainwright	59	14	4	4	1	3	85
Wales	28	0	1	1	6	1	37
Totals	770	40	69	49	92	45	1,065

[a] Harvest year is from July 1 until June 30 of the following year.
Revised April 2, 2001

Table 5. Polar bears tagged by age class, sex, and harvest year[a].

Age	Sex	1987/88-1994/95	1995/96	1996/97	1997/98	1998/99	1999/00	Totals
A	F	71	2	10	11	11	2	107
A	M	205	13	22	13	37	24	314
A	U	10	7	1	0	1	0	19
C	F	14	0	1	1	1	1	18
C	M	24	0	3	1	2	3	33
C	U	4	2	2	1	0	0	9
S	F	50	4	15	9	17	5	100
S	M	112	11	15	13	22	10	183
S	U	5	1	0	0	1	0	7
U	F	88	0	0	0	0	0	88
U	M	157	0	0	0	0	0	157
U	U	30	0	0	0	0	0	30
Totals		770	40	69	49	92	45	1,065

[a] Harvest year is from July 1 until June 30 of the following year.
Age Classes: A = Adult, S = Subadult, C = Cub, U = Unknown
Sex Classes: M = Male, F = Female, U = Unknown
Revised April 2, 2001

Table 6. Walrus tagged, by tagging location and year.

Location	Pre-Rule	1988-95	1996	1997	1998	1999	2000	Totals
Adak	0	0	0	0	1	1	0	2
Anchorage	295	111	8	5	6	12	8	445
Atmautlak	0	0	0	0	0	0	1	1
Barrow	1	121	12	48	22	16	9	229
Bethel	13	91	3	14	13	10	9	153
Brevig Mission	3	43	1	47	107	25	8	234
Chevak	11	18	0	0	0	0	0	29
Chignik	1	0	1	3	0	0	0	5
Chignik Lake	2	0	0	2	0	1	0	5
Clarks Point	8	23	0	0	0	0	0	31
Cold Bay	0	3	0	0	3	0	0	6
Cordova	13	0	0	0	0	1	0	14
Deering	0	0	0	6	0	0	0	6
Dillingham	25	149	63	62	45	16	7	367
Egegik	0	3	3	0	0	0	0	6
Elim	0	8	1	1	0	3	0	13
Emmonak	0	3	0	0	0	0	0	3
Fairbanks	9	6	0	3	6	3	4	31
False Pass	0	0	0	2	0	0	0	2
Gambell	12	3,254	676	353	667	1,058	657	6,677
Golovin	1	6	1	2	4	1	1	16
Goodnews Bay	4	10	1	0	7	3	2	27
Homer	0	6	0	0	0	0	1	7
Hooper Bay	3	31	2	9	8	6	20	79
Kaktovik	0	1	0	0	0	0	0	1
Kenai	2	0	0	0	0	0	3	5
Ketchikan	1	0	0	0	0	0	0	1
King Cove	0	0	0	3	0	0	0	3
King Island	2	472	122	8	12	7	123	746
King Salmon	3	8	2	1	3	2	0	19
Kipnuk	3	13	23	1	6	6	2	54
Kivalina	0	48	12	16	38	13	2	129
Kodiak	2	0	0	0	0	0	2	4
Kongiganak	1	25	5	1	3	3	0	38
Kotzebue	30	3	22	15	2	1	0	73
Koyuk	0	8	0	0	0	0	0	8
Kwigillingok	3	11	1	4	0	0	0	19
Little Diomede	3	1,533	90	152	164	131	145	2,218
Manokotak	3	3	0	0	4	0	0	10
Mekoryuk	23	131	8	13	4	0	6	185
Naknek	3	6	1	0	1	0	0	11
Nelson Lagoon	0	0	0	3	3	1	0	7
Newtok	0	1	0	0	0	0	0	1
Nome	50	109	51	6	17	32	62	327

Table 6. (cont.) Walrus tagged, by tagging location and year.

Location	Pre-Rule	1988-95	1996	1997	1998	1999	2000	Totals
Perryville	0	1	0	0	0	0	0	1
Petersburg	0	0	0	2	0	1	0	3
Pilot Point	0	1	0	3	0	3	1	8
Platinum	20	32	0	14	2	0	0	68
Point Hope	3	23	0	3	1	5	6	41
Point Lay	0	6	4	7	8	6	5	36
Port Heiden	5	15	12	0	0	0	0	32
Quinhagak	0	3	0	0	0	0	0	3
Sand Point	1	10	4	0	0	0	1	16
Savoonga	426	2,351	347	330	297	827	796	5,374
Shaktoolik	0	0	2	0	11	21	3	37
Shishmaref	494	382	66	24	127	28	0	1121
Sitka	15	6	0	0	0	0	0	21
St. George	1	2	0	0	0	0	0	3
St. Michael	0	0	0	0	1	3	0	1
St. Paul	0	10	1	0	0	0	0	11
Stebbins	0	31	0	0	0	0	0	31
Teller	0	19	0	0	9	1	1	3
Togiak	13	120	43	37	40	42	4	299
Toksook Bay	4	11	5	3	3	0	7	33
Tuntutuliak	0	14	0	0	6	0	0	20
Tununak	1	1	2	0	2	0	0	6
Twin Hills	0	0	0	0	0	0	11	11
Unalakleet	6	15	0	0	0	1	0	22
Wainwright	4	318	24	49	69	48	31	543
Wales	10	127	1	2	21	3	14	178
Totals	1,533	9,756	1,618	1,257	1,742	2,341	1,952	20,199

Revised April 2, 2001

Table 7. Walrus tagged by age class, sex, and year.

Age	Sex	Pre-Rule	1988-95	1996	1997	1998	1999	2000	Totals
A	F	236	4,013	637	461	680	1,304	1,073	8,404
A	M	608	4,092	700	684	883	830	680	8,477
A	U	585	538	56	47	79	47	55	1,407
C	F	0	63	0	0	1	0	0	64
C	M	0	63	0	0	0	0	0	63
C	U	1	700	155	35	16	110	74	1,091
S	F	5	53	16	4	11	14	23	126
S	M	27	189	39	22	64	31	40	412
S	U	49	38	15	4	8	5	7	126
U	U	22	7	0	0	0	0	0	29
Totals		1,533	9,756	1,618	1,257	1,742	2,341	1,952	20,199

Age Classes: A = Adult, S = Subadult, C = Calf, U = Unknown
Sex Classes: M = Male, F = Female, U = Unknown
Revised April 2, 2001

Sea Otter-Southern

Sea otters historically ranged throughout the north Pacific from Hokkaido, Japan, through the Aleutian Islands, the Alaskan peninsula, and south along the Pacific coast to Baja California, Mexico. In the mid-1700s, sea otters were recognized as a valuable fur-bearing animal and were subject to an intense commercial harvest. By the early 1900s, the species had been extirpated from most of its historic range except for 13 remnant populations, including one numbering approximately 50 individuals in central California. This remnant population in the near-shore waters of California is referred to as the southern sea otter, and was first recognized as a subspecies in 1904. The historical sea otter population size in California is estimated to have numbered 16,000-18,000 individuals. The Service listed the southern sea otter as threatened under the ESA in 1977 because of its small population size, limited distribution, and its risk of exposure to oil spills throughout its range. Although traditionally the mostserious threat to the southern sea otter was a major oil spill from a tanker in the waters in the vicinity of its range, factors responsible for the declining population counts from 1995-1999 are currently also of great concern.

Standardized population surveys that began in 1982 have continued. The USGS/BRD, the CDFG, the Service and other supporting organizations conducted spring and fall population surveys of the California coast in 1999 and 2000. Spring counts are consistently higher than fall counts, and this is thought to be the result of more favorable sighting conditions in the spring than in the fall. In 1999, the area between Point San Pedro, San Mateo County, and Rincon Point, Santa Barbara County, was surveyed. The 1999 spring survey yielded a count of 2,090 individuals (Table 8) with animals ranging from Pillar Point, San Mateo County, to Carpinteria, Santa Barbara County. In addition, a group of approximately 150 sea otters moved into the Management Zone and was distributed along the Santa Barbara County coast south and east of Point Conception. Five sea otters were also observed at San Miguel Island in the fall. Based on the spring 1999 survey, the total sea otter count was 1.1 percent below the spring 1998 count and down about 12 percent from the peak count in 1995 (Table 8). As in 1998, most otters were sighted between Ano Nuevo, San Mateo County and Point Arguello, Santa Barbara County. Concern over the declining population counts was heightened by three consecutive years of record high mortality, as indicated by beached sea otter carcasses.A total of 2,317 individuals were counted during the 2000 spring survey with animals ranging from Pillar Point Harbor, San Mateo County, to Tajiguas, Santa Barbara County. Based on the spring 2000 survey, the total sea otter count is 10.9 percent above the spring 1999 count. These survey results are encouraging, with the number of southern sea otters counted approaching the highest recorded count for the population. More survey data are needed, however, to determine whether the spring 2000 count is an anomaly or the beginning of a positive trend in southern sea otter population growth.

Southern sea otters

Table 8. Comparison of Sea Otter Counts Conducted Since Spring 1982.
(In 1992, all survey data since Fall 1982 was revied and counts corrected).

Season		Number of Independent Otters	Number of Pups	Total
1982	Spring	1,124	222	1,346
	Fall	1,204	147	1,351
1983	Spring	1,156	121	1,277
	Fall	1,060	163	1,223
1984	Spring	1,180	123	1,303
	Spring*	1,151	52	1,203
	Fall	No survey		
1985	Spring	1,119	242	1,361
	Fall	1,065	150	1,215
1986	Winter**	1,231	181	1,412
	Spring	1,358	228	1,586
	Fall	1,091	113	1,204
1987	Spring	1,435	226	1,661
	Fall	1,260	110	1,370
1988	Spring	1,504	221	1,725
	Fall	No Survey		
1989	Spring	1,571	285	1,856
	Fall	1,492	115	1,607
1990	Spring	1,466	214	1,680
	Fall	1,516	120	1,636
1991	Spring	1,700	241	1,941
	Fall	1,523	138	1,661
1992	Spring	1,810	291	2,101
	Fall	1,581	134	1,715
1993	Spring	2,022	217	2,239
	Fall	1,662	143	1,805
1994	Spring	2,076	283	2,359
	Fall	1,730	115	1,845
1995	Spring	2,095	282	2,377
	Fall	2,053	137	2,190
1996	Spring	1,963	315	2,278
	Fall	1,858	161	2,019
1997	Spring	1,919	310	2,229
	Fall	2,008	197	2,205
1998	Spring	1,955	159	2,114
	Fall	1,726	211	1,937
1999	Spring	1,858	232	2,090
	Fall	1,808	162	1,970
2000	Spring	2,053	264	2,317
	Fall	1,678	199	1,877

* California Department of Fish and Game aerial survey with ground truth
 stations
**Experimental

Translocation of Southern Sea Otters

In our 1982 recovery plan for the southern sea otter, we identified the translocation of southern sea otters as an effective and reasonable recovery action, although we acknowledged that a translocated southern sea otter population could impact shellfish fisheries that had developed in areas formerly occupied by southern sea otters. Goals cited in the recovery plan included: minimizing risk from potential oil spills; establishing at least one additional breeding colony outside the then-current southern sea otter range; and compiling and evaluating information on historical distribution and abundance, available but unoccupied habitat, and potential fishery conflicts.

Public Law 99-625 provided the authority and established the guidelines for carrying out the translocation program. The regulations designating the colony as an experimental population (50 CFR 17.84) established the boundaries of a Translocation Zone to which otters would be translocated and given protection similar to that of the source population, and a Management Zone to be maintained otter-free by nonlethal means.

Between 1987 and 1990, 140 southern sea otters (32 males, 108 females) were translocated to San Nicolas Island, offshore southern California, in an effort to establish a second breeding colony. Through 1999, sea otter surveys were conducted at San Nicolas Island every 2-3 months by the USGS/BRD. During 1999, counts of independent otters ranged from 16 to 21, with 21 being the highest number of independent sea otters counted at San Nicolas Island since September 1989. From the beginning of the translocation program through the end of 2000, a total of 60 pups are known to have been born at the island. Because pups are not marked, an assessment of recruitment into the population was difficult to ascertain.

The purpose of the translocation program was to establish southern sea otters in one or more areas outside the otters' then-current range to minimize the possibility of a single natural or human-caused catastrophe, such as an oil spill, adversely affecting a significant portion of the population. Ultimately, it was anticipated that translocation would result in a larger population size and a more continuous distribution of animals throughout the southern sea otter's former historical range. We viewed translocation as important to achieve recovery and to identify the optimum sustainable population level for the southern sea otter as required under the MMPA.

In March 1999, we distributed a draft evaluation of our translocation program to interested parties. The draft document included the recommendation that we declare the translocation program a failure because fewer than 25 sea otters remained in the translocation zone and reasons for the translocated otters' emigration or mortality could not be identified and/or remedied. We received substantive comments from agencies and the public following release of the draft for review. Comments included both support and lack of support for declaring the translocation program a failure. The majority of respondents cited new information that became available after publication of the EIS for the program. Many respondents encouraged us to look at alternatives not identified in the EIS or corresponding implementing regulations.

We prepared a draft biological opinion evaluating southern sea otter containment and distributed it to interested parties for comment on March 19, 1999. On July 19, 2000, we completed a final opinion. Our reinitiation of consultation was prompted by the receipt of substantial new information on the population status, behavior, and ecology of the southern sea otter that revealed effects of containment that were not previously considered. Specifically, the biological opinion noted that in 1998 and 1999 southern sea otters moved into the management zone in much greater numbers than had occurred in prior years; analysis of carcasses indicated that southern sea otters were being exposed to environmental contaminants and diseases which could be affecting the health of the population throughout California; range-wide counts of southern sea otters found numbers were declining; recent information, in particular the implications of the effects of the Exxon Valdez oil spill, indicated that sea otters at San Nicolas Island would not be isolated from the potential effects of a single large oil spill; and the capture of large groups of sea otters in the management zone and subsequent release into the parent population was likely to result in substantial adverse effects on the parent population. We concluded that reversal of the southern sea otter population decline and expansion of the southern sea otter's population distribution are essential to its survival and recovery. We further concluded that continuation of the containment program, while restricting the southern sea otter to the area north of Point Conception, will likely exacerbate recent sea otter population declines and increase vulnerability to a catastrophic oil spill or other man-made or natural stochastic events, and, therefore, likely jeopardize the continued existence of the species.

On February 8, 2000, a draft revised recovery plan for the southern sea otter was released for public review and comment (65 FR 6221). Based on the observed decline in abundance and shift in distribution of the southern sea otter population, the recovery team recommended in the draft revised recovery plan that it would be in the best interest of the southern sea otter to declare the experimental translocation of southern sea otters to San Nicolas Island a failure and discontinue maintenance of the management zone. The recovery team's recommendation will be fully evaluated through our ongoing NEPA process on the translocation action.

Incidental Take Within the Mainland Range

Several lines of direct and indirect evidence indicate that incidental drowning of sea otters in gill and trammel entangling nets has been a significant source of mortality in past years. The State of California entered into a cooperative agreement with the NMFS to assist with the monitoring program required under the 1988 amendments to the Act. In Monterey Bay and Morro Bay, up to three NMFS observers had been stationed to document incidental take, although no observers were used in 1998. From June 1982 to December 31, 2000, 76 southern sea otters were observed or otherwise known to have drowned in legally set commercial fishing nets.

On September 13, 2000, the Director of the CDFG issued an order to close the halibut gillnet fishery in waters less than 60 fathoms (360 feet) in depth from Marin County southward throughout Monterey Bay, and between Point Sal and Point Arguello in northern Santa Barbara County. The order was prompted by concern for common murre (a sea bird) and sea otter populations. We believe that this and other State legislation has significantly reduced the number of sea otters drowned in gill nets.

The crab, lobster, and fish trap fisheries continue to be a concern as a source of mortality for otters. Sparse data and anecdotal records indicate that southern sea otters are incidentally taken in these fisheries. Sea otters are known to be taken occasionally in Alaska's crab pot fishery. However, Alaska's pot fishery uses different types of gear and is not directly comparable to the California fishery. In recent years, the fish trap fishery increased along the California coast. Traps for fish are set within the kelp beds near shore in the same areas sea otters prefer to forage. A USGS/BRD study investigating the potential for sea otter entrapment in fish traps was completed in 2000. The results of the study, which was initially begun and conducted in a controlled environment, indicate that sea otters do enter traps and can become trapped in this type of fishing gear. The CDFG is now considering trap modifications for the fishery to prevent incidental take of sea otters.

Sea Otter Mortality
Over 100 sea otter carcasses wash ashore every year. In 1999, 187 southern sea otter carcasses were recovered from beaches. This represents the second highest number of recovered beach cast carcasses and is equivalent to 8.9 percent of the spring count. The previous record of 213 carcasses was set in 1998 (10.1 percent of the spring count). In 2000, 153 southern sea otters were recovered from California's beaches, representing 6.6 percent of the 2000 spring count.

The National Wildlife Health Center (NWHC) has conducted necropsies on fresh, beach cast sea otter carcasses since 1992. The immediate goals of this program are to identify the major causes of death in sea otters and to establish their relative frequencies. In 2000, the necropsy program at the NWHC continued at the same level of coverage as in 1997, 1998 , and 1999. Approximately 25 percent of fresh carcasses recovered were necropsied by NWHC with the remainder of those necropsied done so by CDFG. Causes of death among necropsied animals have not significantly changed since 1992 when most sea otter deaths were attributed to infectious diseases (42 percent). These diseases include coccidioidomycosis, acanthocephalan peritonitis, protozoal encephalitis, and other diseases. Other sources of mortality include various types of trauma (shark bite, lacerations, etc.), emaciation, tumors, and various conditions of mechanical or functional impairment (esophageal impaction, intestinal perforation, intestinal volvulus, etc.). The USGS/BRD received funding in 2000 to study the causes of observed declines through 1999 in population counts of southern sea otters including an assessment and identification of sources of mortality. During 1999, a record number of white shark-bitten sea otter carcasses was recovered (33, or 18 percent of the total).

Stranding and Rehabilitation Program
The Monterey Bay Aquarium is the

primary facility involved in the rescue and rehabilitation of stranded southern sea otters. In 1994, the Service authorized a second facility, The Marine Mammal Center of Sausalito, California, to rescue and rehabilitate stranded southern sea otters for the purpose of returning them to the wild.

Rehabilitated sea otters that lack the skills to survive in the wild are placed in permanent housing in a number of facilities. By 2000, these facilities included the Monterey Bay Aquarium, Sea World of San Diego, Oregon Zoo, Oregon Coast Aquarium, Ocean Journey (Denver), New England Aquarium, New York Aquarium, Aquarium of the Americas (New Orleans), and Aquarium of the Pacific (Long Beach).

ESA Section 7 Consultations
Pursuant to Section 7 of the ESA, we review proposed Federally funded, conducted, or permitted activities that may affect the southern sea otter. In 1999, we reinitiated consultation on continuing the containment program, established as part of the Southern Sea Otter Translocation Program. In July 2000, we completed this intra-Service consultation and issued a biological opinion, finding that continuing the containment program would jeopardize the continued existence of the species (see section on Translocation of Southern Sea Otters above).

Oil Spill Activities
The Service's sea otter oil spill contingency plan is still in draft and needs to be revised to incorporate pertinent aspects of the Federal Oil Pollution Act of 1990, and California Senate Bill #2040 which created a new oil spill division within the CDFG. Ramifications of both Federal and State legislation has yet to be realized or applied to the existing document.

The CDFG's Office of Spill Prevention and Response has developed area contingency plans for oil spill in California as well as a wildlife response plan that includes special procedures for handling of sea otters in the event of a spill. The sea otter oil spill contingency plan is incorporated into the existing plans and is periodically updated, most recently in 1999. No oil spills affected southern sea otters in 1999 and 2000.

Three restoration projects have been selected and the projects began early in 1999. The projects are: (1) Establishing the Factors That Affect Survivability of Wild and Rehabilitated Sea Otters; (2) Baseline Health Studies: Part I: Baseline Health Studies on Southern Sea Otters and Comparison to Otters

Injured in the Avila Beach Unocal Spill; and (3) Part II: Analysis and Comparison of Existing Blood Samples for Polycyclic Aromatic Hydrocarbons (PAH) by Enzyme-Linked Immunosorbent Assay (ELISA) and Gas Chromatography Mass Spectroscopy (GCMS). A copy of the final restoration plan is available from the Land Conservancy of San Luis Obispo County's web page (http://www.slonet.org/vv/land_con).

Sea Otter-Northern (Washington State Population)
The northern sea otter (Enhydra lutris kenyoni) historically inhabited the ocean waters off the coast of Washington State; however, little information exists on population size and the exact distribution. It is believed that otter populations were diminished to low numbers primarily as a result of the maritime fur trade in the mid 1800s. The species was probably extirpated from the State by the early 20th century (Schaffer 1940). In 1969 and 1970, as the result of a joint effort between the Washington Department of Fish and Wildlife, the ADFG, the Department of Defense, and the Service to reestablish the species, a total of 59 otters were brought to the Washington coast from Amchitka Island in the central Aleutian Islands of Alaska (Jameson et al., 1982).

The reintroduced population was not surveyed between 1970 and 1977. In 1977, the Service surveyed the coast and counted only 19 sea otters. The population was surveyed again in 1978, every other year from 1981 through 1989; and annually since 1989 using combined aerial and ground counts (Table 9). Based on the 2000 summer survey (actual count), the minimum size of this population is 504 animals, a 17 percent decrease below the 1999 count of 605. The average finite rate of increase for this population since 1989 is 9.4 percent. Until recently, the population rarely dispersed far from their core range of Neah Bay south to Destruction Island. Currently the population is showing signs of range expansion, moving into the Straits of Juan De Fuca and down the outer coast of Washington.

The Washington population of sea otters is protected under the MMPA, but is not afforded additional protection under the ESA. In 1981, the Washington Department of Fish and Wildlife designated the sea otter as State endangered. In 2000, the Service participated in the development of the Draft Washington State Recovery Plan for the Northern Sea Otter.

Sea Otter Mortality

Several factors have been identified which may cause sea otter mortality in Washington including oil spills, other contaminants, marine biotoxins, entanglement and entrapment in nets, habitat loss, and disturbance. Since their reintroduction in 1969-70, a few sea otter carcasses have been reported annually, but sources of human-caused mortality affecting this population is not well documented. Sea otters are susceptible to drowning in gill nets in Washington's coastal gill net fisheries conducted by tribal fishermen, but documented incidental takes are rare. At least three sea otters are reported to have been killed in a tribal fishery for chinook salmon set-net in the vicinity of Point of the Arches on the north Washington coast in 1996. As the Washington sea otter population moves east and south, the probability of fisheries-related incidental take will increase.

In 2000, a total of 22 carcasses were reported from May 2 through August 16, with the majority of carcasses being reported between late June and mid August. In an effort to determine the cause of this abnormally high mortality, seven of these animals were collected and necropsy was performed. At the time of this report, a definitive cause of death had not been established for six of these animals. One animal was determined to have protozoal encephalitis. Laboratory results received thus far indicate that the deaths were likely acute and not related to a chronic condition. At this time the Service is awaiting further test results, including tests evaluating environmental contaminant levels in the liver tissue of these animals.

Several Native Americans of the Pacific northwest have treaty reserved hunting and fishing rights. The Makah tribe has asserted that their reserved hunting rights apply to sea otters. Currently, there is no harvest of sea otters by the Makah tribe, although they have informally expressed an interest in possibly developing such a program.

Oil Spill Activities

In the past decade two oil spills have occurred within the range of the northern sea otter population in Washington, however, only one documented oil-related death was recorded during either of the spills. With the volume of shipping traffic into, and out of, the Strait of Juan de Fuca the potential for a catastrophic spill event still exists and the population is vulnerable to the effects of such a spill.

Table 9. Northern Sea Otter Population Numbers in Washington State, 1989- 2000

Year	Population Size
1989	208
1990	212
1991	276
1992	313
1993	307
1994	360
1995	395
1996	430
1997	502
1998	433
1999	605
2000	504

The Service currently has both national and regional oil spill response contingency plans in place, including a sea otter response plan. In addition, we have developed a sea otter rescue protocol for the state of Washington and would work in conjunction with the State during oil spill events.

Research

In FY 2000, the Service, in cooperation with the USGS/BRD, the Olympic Coast National Marine Sanctuary, the National Marine Mammal Laboratory, Alaska Fisheries Science Center, and the Washington Department of Fish and Wildlife, funded a study to estimate the sea otter carrying capacity of the Washington coast. The results of this study are expected in 2001.

References

Jameson, R .J., K. W. Kenyon, A.M. Johnson, and H.M. Wight. 1982. History and status of translocated sea otter populations in North America. Wildlife Society Bulletin 10: 100-07.

Schaffer, V.B. 1940. The sea otter on the Washington coast. Pacific Northwest Quarterly 10:370-388.

West Indian Manatee

The West Indian maperception, the manatee was first afforded protection by the State of Florida in 1893. It is now variously protected by the State of Florida's Manatee Sanctuary Act of 1978, the ESA, and the MMPA.natee in Florida represents the northernmost and largest remaining component of a manatee population once found throughout the Caribbean basin. Physically isolated from its counterparts, the manatee in Florida has historically been viewed as rare and declining in number. Because of this Manatee research and management initiatives over the past 30 years have shown that the manatee's future depends upon a better understanding of its status and life history and on better protecting the manatee and its habitat from direct and indirect impacts. The protection of these essential components in the face of an increasing human population, development, and use of watercraft underscores the need to continue to balance the needs of the manatee with its human neighbors.

As a Federally listed endangered species, efforts to recover the species are guided by the manatee recovery program, through the Division of Ecological Services. This program, through the revised Florida Manatee Recovery Plan of 1996, coordinates Federal, State, local and private manatee recovery efforts. Recovery activities incorporate both research and management efforts. Research efforts have focused on monitoring the status of the manatee and its habitat, and on better defining various components of its life history. Management initiatives have concentrated on protecting essential manatee habitat and reducing human-related causes of manatee mortality. Our field offices that play an integral role in the manatee recovery process include the Jacksonville and Vero Beach field offices, and various National Wildlife Refuges located within the range of the Florida manatee.

Status

While most authorities agree that the present size of the manatee population has increased over the past few decades, the extent to which this has occurred is unknown. It has been suggested that this growth may be attributed, in part, to a number of factors including but not limited to the cessation of hunting, an abundance of native and exotic food plants, the relatively recent existence of nonnatural warm water refuges, the establishment and enforcement of manatee protection zones, and public education.

The Florida Fish and Wildlife Conservation Commission (FFWCC), formerly the Florida Game and Freshwater Fish Commission, coordinates a series of synoptic aerial surveys and ground counts during peak cold periods when manatees tend to aggregate in warm water locations. The surveys focus on these warm water aggregation sites and are used to assess manatee abundance. Surveys conducted between 1991 and 1998 produced high counts that ranged from 1,465 to 2,639

Manatee surfacing to breathe

animals. Three Statewide surveys were flown in 1999. The surveys, flown on January 6, February 23, and March 6, 1999, yielded counts of 1,873 manatees, 2,034 manatees, and 2,353 manatees, respectively. Statewide counts on January 16 and 27, 2000, differed by 36 on January 16 and 27, 2000, differed by 36 percent, at 1,629 and 2,222, respectively; while the synoptic survey in January 2001 resulted in a count of 3,276 animals, the highest count to date. The highest previous count was 2,639 in 1996. Survey results are highly variable and do not reflect an actual population trend. Excellent survey conditions and an unusually cold winter undoubtedly contributed to the high count in 2001. While population biologists have used this information to model trends, the exact number of manatees in Florida is unknown. Manatees are difficult to count because they are often in areas with poor water clarity, and their behavior (such as resting on the bottom of a deep canal) may make them difficult to see.

Long-term studies suggest that there are four relatively distinct regional subpopulations of the Florida manatee: Northwest, Southwest, Atlantic (including the St. Johns River north of Palatka), and St. Johns River (south of Palatka). These divisions are based primarily on documented manatee use of wintering sites and from radio tracking studies of individuals' movements. Although some movement occurs among subpopulations, researchers have found that analysis of manatee status on a regional level provided insights into important factors related to manatee recovery.

Evidence indicates that the Northwest

and Upper St. Johns River subpopulations have steadily increased over the last 25 years. This population growth is consistent with the lower number of human-related deaths, high estimates of adult survival, and good manatee habitat in these regions. This good news is tempered by the fact that the manatees in these two regions probably account for less than 20 percent of the State's manatee population.

The picture is less optimistic for the Atlantic coast subpopulation. Scientists are concerned that the adult survival rate (i.e., the percentage of adults that survives from one year to the next) is lower than what is needed for sustained population growth. The population on this coast appears to have been growing slowly in the 1980s but may now have leveled off, or could even be declining. This finding is consistent with the high level of human-related and, in some years, cold-related mortality in the region.

Estimates of survival and population growth rates are currently underway for the Southwest region. Preliminary estimates of adult survival are similar to those for the Atlantic region, i.e., substantially lower than those for the Northwest and Upper St. Johns River regions. This area has had high levels of watercraft-related deaths and injuries, as well as periodic natural mortality events caused by red tide and severe cold. However, pending further data collection and analysis, scientists are unable to provide an assessment of how manatees are doing in this part of the State.

Over the past ten years, approximately

30 percent of manatee deaths have been directly attributable to human-related causes, including watercraft collisions, accidental crushing and drowning in water control structures, and entanglements in fishing gear. A total of 274 manatees died in 1999. Included in these mortalities were 83 manatees that died from watercraft collisions, 15 crushed and killed in flood gates and water control structures, and 8 that died from other human-related causes. This was the worst year on record for total number of watercraft-related manatee deaths. In 2000, 34 percent (94 of 273) of manatee deaths were human-related. Included were 78 manatees that died from watercraft collisions, 8 crushed and killed in flood gates and water control structures, and 8 that died from other human-related causes. This was the second worst year on record for total number of watercraft-related manatee deaths.

We (and subsequently the State of Florida and its contractors) began examining manatee carcasses in 1974. Between 1976 and 2000, 4,082 manatee carcasses have been recovered. Of these, 990 (24 percent) have died from collisions with watercraft, 168 (4 percent) have died in water control structures, and 112 (3 percent) have died from other human-related causes (e.g., entanglements in and ingestion of fishing gear, entrapment in stormwater pipes). The continued high level of manatee deaths raises concern about the ability of the overall population to grow or at least remain stable. The negative impacts of factors that are difficult to quantify, such as habitat loss and chronic effects of severe injuries, are also a concern. Adult survival is critical to the manatee's recovery. In the regions where adult survival rates are high, the population has grown at a healthy rate. In order to assure high adult survival, recovery efforts need to significantly reduce the number of human-related manatee deaths.

Management
Manatees and their behavior and habitat have been closely monitored for more than 25 years through the carcass salvage program, photo identification studies, aerial surveys, tracking projects, and other studies. These data have been used to track the status of the manatee population and to assist Federal, State, and local agencies in their efforts to protect manatees from direct threats such as watercraft and water control structures, and from indirect threats such as habitat loss.

Since 1978, management efforts to reduce human-related manatee deaths have included strategies focused on reducing manatee collisions with boats, reducing hazards such as entrapment in water control structures and entanglement in fishing gear, and protecting manatee winter aggregation sites to reduce cold-related mortality. Managers are continually challenged to develop innovative protection strategies, given the rapidly growing human population along Florida's coasts and resultant rangewide impacts to manatees and their habitat.

An important focus of our efforts to recover the manatee is to improve compliance with manatee protection zones. The zones, some of which were first designated in 1978, require boat operators to drive their boats at slow or idle speeds in sensitive manatee areas. Manatees are capable of hearing boats and can, and do, get out of their way, if they are given time to do so. Compliance with speed zones will minimize the number of manatees that die in these areas. To promote compliance, Service law enforcement officers implemented seven law enforcement task force initiatives in 1999. These initiatives, conducted in sensitive manatee areas, cited 749 boat operators for violating speed zone restrictions. These efforts were enhanced by the USCG, which made 697 cases in 1999.

Water Control Structures
Water control structures are a persistent source of human-related manatee mortality. Members of an interagency task force that includes the Army Corps of Engineers (Corps), the South Florida Water Management District, the Florida Fish and Wildlife Conservation Commission, and others have taken steps to reduce the number of animals killed in these structures every year. Efforts include refitting flood control gates with pressure sensitive devices and navigation lock doors with acoustic sensors; both devices stop gate and lock closures when manatees are present, thereby reducing the number of animals crushed in these devices each year. Four flood gate structures (10 gates) and 2 navigation locks have been equipped with these devices since 1997. The Canaveral Locks were fitted in 2000. Preliminary test results were encouraging. However, in 1999, two manatees died in flood gates and one died in a navigation lock. Installation flaws were implicated in all of these deaths and steps have been taken to correct these problems. The Rodman Dam and Reservoir in Putnam County, Florida, have been a chronic source of structure-related mortality for many years. In 1999, the Service advocated a refit of navigation locks and spillway gates to protect manatees as a

stop gap measure and recommended to the State that a preferred alternative would be to remove the dam. Additionally, eight manatees died in water control structures in 2000.

Industrial Warm Water Discharges
Historically, Florida manatees relied on natural warm water springs and coastal waters in the southern part of the State for warmth during critical cold winter periods. The development of warm water discharges at power and manufacturing plants in the first half of the 20th century provided manatees with alternative wintering sites, including some well north of their traditional wintering range. Today, more than half of the manatee population relies on industrial warm water discharges for warmth during the winter. The Service, in conjunction with the Environmental Protection Agency, and the FFWCC, has encouraged the elimination of these artificial warm water sites in coastal Georgia and northeast Florida. Plants to the south, where most of these animals winter, are currently in operation; these plants are older, less efficient, and are not necessarily reliable during critical winter periods. Efforts to deregulate the power industry will influence the viability of these sites. Given these concerns, the Service held a two-day workshop in 1999 to review the status of the manatees' winter habitat, to identify threats, and to identify ways to protect these areas and the manatees that use them. The Service is creating a task force to address these concerns and to take steps to ensure the safety of manatees that use these sites.

Manatee Rescue, Rehabilitation, and Release Activities
Service biologists coordinated a manatee rescue, rehabilitation, and release program in 1999 and 2000 to treat injured and distressed manatees. The program aids recovery efforts by assisting distressed manatees and reintroducing them into the wild, and by drawing attention to the species through outreach inherent in the program. In 1999, a total of 44 manatees were rescued and ten were released. At year's end, 54 manatees were in captivity for treatment, including animals receiving long-term care. The Service authorizes 18 private organizations and works with other permitted State and Federal organizations to help these animals. The program largely relies on these organizations to fund these activities. Manatee rescues, captive manatees, and manatee releases draw attention to the manatee and the problems that they face. The media heavily publicize rescues and releases and more than 10,000,000 visitors a year see manatees

at critical and long-term care facilities; manatees maintained in captivity may be viewed by the public, provided their display does not impede their recovery.

In 2000, 46 manatees were rescued and 32 were released (including 13 that were treated in the field and subsequently released). Fifty-seven manatees were in captivity for treatment at the end of 2000, including animals receiving long-term care. Florida's State legislature budgeted funds in 2000 to help offset costs incurred by these organizations in carrying out these activities.

Outreach and Education
Service manatee outreach and education efforts during the 1999-2000 time period included preparing hundreds of written responses to persons seeking information about manatees and the distribution of thousands of brochures and handouts through correspondence and public meetings. Service biologists routinely review, prepare comments on, and develop outreach materials promoting manatee conservation. Numerous interviews are given each year to the media, and presentations are made to various schools and outreach groups. Refuge outreach programs have been a particularly effective tool by which refuge visitors learn about manatees, manatee refuges, and manatee conservation. The Service's manatee law enforcement coordinator developed a presentation to promote law enforcement efforts; USCG personnel at stations throughout Florida have received training to enhance compliance with manatee protection zones. In 2000, the Service helped to prepare and fund a new waterproof boater's card, "Mind Your Waterway Signs" and designed an outreach display.

Service efforts in 2000 to protect manatees were complicated as we were inundated with questions and concerns raised by issues involved in the lawsuit. In addition, rumors and misinformation abounded regarding manatees and manatee protection efforts. Common misconceptions included statements to the effect that manatees were an invasive, nonnative species; that manatee protection would preclude access by waterfront property owners and would result in a severe decrease in property values; and that vast areas of coastal and inland waters would be closed to all public access. Service personnel fielded questions about these concerns from hundreds of reporters and thousands of citizens.

One of the Service's most important outreach tools is the manatee rescue, rehabilitation, and release program.

Manatee rescues, captive manatees, and manatee releases draw attention to the manatee and the problems that they face. (Manatees maintained in captivity may be viewed by the public, provided their display does not impede their rehabilitation). The media heavily publicize rescues and releases and more than 10 million visitors a year see manatees at critical and long-term care facilities. The 10 facilities housing manatees provide manatee recovery efforts with one of the most valuable and far-reaching educational tools for manatee conservation. These facilities do an outstanding job of interpreting the challenges that face manatees and do a great deal to promote a constituency for the species.

Lawsuit
On May 20, 1999, the Service received a Notice of Intent to Sue from the Save the Manatee Club and 21 other environmental organizations for alleged violations of Federal statutes that protect the Florida manatee. In particular, the notice identified concerns related to: (1) the development of recovery plans, (2) the development of biological opinions, and (3) a purported failure to prepare environmental impact statements and assessments on the cumulative effect of development projects in manatee habitat. The notice proposed solutions to these perceived deficiencies, including the: (1) development of objective, measurable criteria for down- and de-listing the Florida manatee; (2) effective implementation of manatee protection zones; (3) creation of a network of sanctuaries and refuges; and (4) issuance of jeopardy biological opinions for projects that will result in increasing boat traffic. Responses were prepared to address these concerns.

On January 13, 2000, the Save the Manatee Club and 17 other environmental organizations, as well as three individuals, filed suit against the Service and the Corps. The lawsuit charged the Service and the Corps of allegedly violating Federal statutes that protect the Florida manatee. (A similar lawsuit was filed against the State's Fish and Wildlife Conservation Commission, alleging that the State was in violation of Federal laws.) By the end of the 2000, the Service, Corps, plaintiffs, and intervenors in the Federal lawsuit agreed to settle. Under terms of the settlement agreement, the Service agreed to time frames for completing a number of manatee conservation activities. These activities include revising the manatee recovery plan, establishing new Federal manatee protection areas, and pursuing regulations to allow for incidental take of manatees under Section 101(a)(5)(A)

of the Act. In addition, the Service and the Corps agreed to revise procedures for reviewing permit applications for the construction of boating facilities in manatee habitat.

Review of Federal Actions
Historically, we have relied on section 7 of the ESA to minimize the effects of boat facility development on manatees and their habitat. In 2000, most section 7 reviews of development projects that could affect manatees were delayed due to the lawsuit. During this time, we reevaluated the use of section 7 as a means to minimize the effect of such projects on manatees. As a result of this reevaluation, we drafted interim guidance for the section 7 process and made plans to further address takings issues through the MMPA's incidental take provisions.

The interim guidance applies to actions that may result in increased watercraft access in Florida. It identifies conditions which will allow the Service to determine when a proposed watercraft access facility is unlikely to have adverse indirect effects on manatees as well as the measures that an individual seeking authorization to build a watercraft access facility could take to reduce indirect effects on manatees to an "unlikely to occur" level. These interim measures will be used until the Service completes its promulgation of incidental take regulations under the Act.

Pursuant to plans to address takings issues through the Act's incidental take provisions, the Service plans to request authorization to "take" small numbers of Florida manatees. In Florida, county, State, and Federal agencies engage in a variety of activities that may result in the incidental, unintentional take of manatees by watercraft. Many of these activities relate to the use and regulation of watercraft operated in Florida waters

accessible to manatees, including: (1) regulating boater behavior on the water (e.g., speed zones and vessel registration); (2) permitting construction of watercraft access facilities (i.e., marinas, docks, boat ramps); (3) funding construction of watercraft access facilities; (4) operating watercraft access facilities; and (5) operating watercraft. To date, there is no authorization for the incidental, unintentional death, injury, or harassment of manatees caused by these otherwise legal activities. The Service engages in, or has the authority to engage in, each of the above five categories of activities; therefore, Service activities could result in the incidental, unintentional take of manatees. As such, the Service plans to request development of incidental take regulations for Service activities and to promulgate regulations to allow authorization of a small amount of take associated with government activities related to watercraft in Florida. Through this rule-making the Service will determine whether take associated with watercraft use and regulation in Florida will have a negligible impact on manatees, after taking into account mitigating measures that would render the impact negligible when it may not otherwise meet that standard.

To improve the project evaluation process, the Corps prepared a series of GIS coverages that include known manatee habitat in Florida. These provide project reviewers with a more effective means to evaluate manatees and their habitats in the context of permitting and development activities. The program divides the State into 80 discreet areas or reaches with overlays that include area manatee data, habitat information, development locations, and other sources of information. This tool will help to identify potential problem areas as well as areas with adequate protection for manatees.

Manatee with scars

Robert K. Boone/USFWS

Manatee Protection Areas

In order to minimize the number of manatees struck and killed or harassed by watercraft, manatees are protected through a network of manatee protection areas. These areas, designated by both State and Federal agencies, protect manatees by limiting boat speeds and access in important manatee use areas. By slowing boats, manatees are given ample time to get out of the way of moving boats and thus avoid collisions. Furthermore, limited access areas prevent manatee disturbance caused by boats and other activities in especially sensitive use areas, including warm water refuges.

In 2000, Florida finalized rules adopting manatee protection zones in Lee and Duval Counties. To date, the State has adopted rules in 22 Florida counties. Where appropriate, the Service endorses State rules and has the authority to enforce these areas when they are appropriately marked. The Service has not endorsed the newly adopted zones in Duval County, citing the inadequacy of these measures to effectively protect manatees and the fact that the newly designated zones are unenforceable.

An Advance Notice of Rulemaking was published in the Federal Register in September 2000 advising the public that the Service planned to designate manatee refuges and sanctuaries. As part of this process, Service personnel met with Federal, State, and local managers and planners involved in manatee protection, law enforcement officers and manatee researchers in an effort to preliminarily identify sites important to manatees that are currently lacking adequate protection. Five meetings were held with these experts, one in each quadrant of Florida and a meeting to evaluate coastal Georgia. As a result of these meetings, approximately 150 individual sites were identified. Following this effort, the Service hosted six public information meetings (at Crystal River, St. Petersburg, Ft. Myers, Miami, Viera, and Palatka) in December 2000 to solicit comments and suggestions regarding these sites, as well as any additional recommendations that the public might have.

Law Enforcement Activities

An important focus of Service efforts to recover the manatee is to improve compliance with manatee protection zones. Compliance with speed zones will minimize the number of manatees that die in these areas. To promote compliance, Service law enforcement officers implemented numerous law enforcement task force initiatives during 2000. These initiatives ranged from operations involving numerous officers to smaller efforts dispersed throughout the State. As a result of these efforts, over 800 notices of violation were issued to violators for speeding in manatee zones.

The USCG also played a key role in manatee protection through law enforcement activities. All USCG Stations in peninsular Florida participated in enforcement activities. USCG Boarding Officers issued a total of 645 tickets during 2000 for violations of manatee speed zones. Analyzed by station, this total includes 248 from Station Miami Beach, 188 from Station Ft. Lauderdale, 59 from Station Ponce Inlet, 38 from Station Lake Worth, 34 from Station Yankeetown, 33 from Station Cortez, 19 from Station Ft. Myers, 16 from Station Mayport and 10 from Station Ft. Pierce.

With the extremely high manatee mortality numbers at the start of the year, law enforcement efforts by officers of the FFWCC were intensified. A combined enforcement/education campaign focused on Dade, Brevard, Lee, and Collier Counties, areas that experienced heavy watercraft-related mortality. Manatee protection was also conducted by many county sheriff's offices and local police departments. Among the most active was the Metro-Dade Police Department's Marine Unit. This unit issued several hundred manatee violation tickets during the year.

To gauge the effectiveness of law enforcement efforts and to monitor boater compliance within manatee protection zones, the Service partnered with the FFWCC to conduct boater compliance surveys in various areas throughout the State. Preliminary field assessments were completed in 2000.

Habitat Management

Essential manatee habitat includes foraging and freshwater sites, travel corridors, resting, cavorting, and calving areas, and warm water refuges. These areas are heavily influenced by human activities and must be properly managed to support species recovery. Human impacts include dramatic declines in seagrass area over the past 50 years and drinking sites that have both disappeared and appeared (including new, artificial sites such as storm water runoff pipes and ditches, process water, etc.). The diversion of river courses, damming, construction of canals, shoreline bulkheading, and other activities have altered corridors and use areas which have been further compromised by waterborne activities (e.g., boating) and other disturbances.

Historical warm water refuges, used by wintering manatees, have also been modified. Spring flows have been reduced and/or lost due to groundwater withdrawals and impacts to recharge areas, south Florida ambient waters have been altered due to development activities, and winter distribution patterns have been changed with the addition of industrial warm water outfalls.

To ensure that these changes do not have a significant, adverse effect on manatees, many of these impacts are addressed through various state and Federal permitting programs, as well as through planning groups. The Service relies upon section 7 and Fish and Wildlife Coordination Act reviews to minimize the effect of construction on important use areas. An interagency group ensures that aquatic plant control activities are balanced with the needs of wintering manatees at important winter sites. The Service, through coastal program activities, has been active in efforts to restore grassbeds.

Natural and industrial warm water refuge concerns are being addressed by interim and long range planning. Extant industrial warm water discharges are made safe for manatees through the use of manatee protection plans, included as conditions of NPDES permits. While the future status of these sites is unknown, it is apparent that some will be eliminated and others operated in some diminished capacity. To address these concerns, the Service's Warm Water Task Force, made up of representatives from industry, resource management agencies, research organizations, environmental groups, etc., is reviewing the current network of sites and preparing plans in anticipation of these changes.

The Service was also involved in State activities focused on protecting natural warm water sites. Florida Governor Jeb Bush convened a "Springs Task Force" to develop a management plan for Florida's springs; the Service helped to draft the plan, which is currently in its implementation stage. The State is also involved in maintaining spring flows through legislatively mandated requirements to establish minimum flows in Florida waterbodies. The Service worked closely with the St. Johns River Water Management District to establish minimum flow levels at Blue Spring, a primary warm water refuge for manatees located in the upper St. Johns River.

Entanglements

Every year manatees become entangled in monofilament fishing line, crab trap float lines, and other types of fishing gear. While the majority of these entangled animals are rescued, treated, and released back into the wild through the Service's manatee rescue program, animals occasionally die as a result of complications associated with these events. In 2000, nine manatees were rescued from fishing gear (including two from monofilament line and two from crab trap lines.) Service sponsored research at Sea World's Hubbs Research Institute is investigating the ways in which animals are becoming entangled. This information will be used to promote gear cleanups and possible modifications to fishing gear.

Recovery Planning

A manatee recovery team was convened in 1998 to revise the Florida Manatee Recovery Plan. The team met four times in 1999. Team initiatives included developing updated objective, measurable criteria for defining when Florida manatees should be listed as endangered and threatened under the ESA. The team based criteria (developed by the Manatee Population Status Working Group) on manatee survivorship and reproduction rates. Other recovery team activities included the development of recovery tasks, and a revised draft recovery plan, the completion of which was expected in 2000. The recovery team met several times in 2000 to complete its draft of the third revision of The Florida Manatee Recovery Plan. A draft was completed and made available to the public on November 30, 2000. A final plan was completed in fall 2001.

Summary

In the two years covered by this report, substantial progress was made to enhance the long-term survival prospects of manatees. Recovery team members furthered efforts to reduce watercraft and water control structure-related mortality. Various habitat conservation initiatives promoted and enhanced essential manatee habitat areas. Researchers continued to identify manatee habitat and to assess manatee distribution, abundance, and the status of the manatee.

Hawaiian Monk Seal and Other Marine Mammal Activities on Pacific Islands

Pacific/Remote Islands National Wildlife Refuge Complex Activities

Service personnel from the Hawaiian Islands NWR and Midway Atoll NWR cooperate regularly with NMFS personnel on various research and recovery actions recommended in the Hawaiian Monk Seal Recovery Plan and respond to additional situations involving monk seals as needed. Hawaiian Islands NWR staff provide a variety of support services, including transportation of equipment and supplies aboard Service-funded charters, radio-monitoring and message relays, and maintenance of the Tern Island Field Station. The NMFS maintains seasonal field camps and crews on several islands of the Hawaiian Islands NWR including Tern Island, Laysan Island, Lisianski Island, and Pearl and Hermes Reef. Tern Island and Laysan Island are manned by Service personnel year-round, assisting the monk seal researchers in any way possible while the NMFS camps are present on these islands including assistance in conducting population surveys, production estimates, tagging efforts, resighting of marked seals, and deployment of satellite tags. Midway Atoll NWR also hosts NMFS biologists in support of Hawaiian monk seal research.

Monk seal monitoring efforts in 1999 documented increased juvenile survival at French Frigate Shoals and Lisianski Island, while juvenile survival at other areas remained similar to previous years. The total number of pups born on the six principal pupping areas remained relatively high (n=243), although at least 25 pups were lost to shark predation at French Frigate Shoals.

Service personnel worked with cooperators from the NMFS, the USCG, the State of Hawaii, and others to document and remove net debris from Northwestern Hawaiian Island reefs. More than 25.5 tons of material was collected from Lisianski, Pearl, and Hermes Reef and Midway. A record high of 23 seals were observed entangled in 1999, all of which were freed by observers or escaped on their own. In October 2000, we again participated in a multi-agency reef clean-up during which approximately 25 tons of debris (primarily derelict fishing gear) was removed from Pearl and Hermes Reef, Kure Atoll, Midway Atoll, and the reefs around Lisianski Island. Documented entanglements of Hawaiian monk seals were down from 23 in 1999 to 5 animals in 2000.

During 1999, Service personnel also assisted NMFS and other cooperators in movement of 10 captive seals to SeaWorld/San Antonio, studies of shark predation at French Frigate Shoals, and collection of monk seal prey for fatty acid analysis. Service personnel also assisted on a health assessment project involving monk seals at several atolls and islands. Preliminary results of this assessment do not preclude future translocation of weaned pups from French Frigate Shoals to Midway, a potential recovery action to be considered in the future.

The Service, working with NMFS, USCG, and other cooperators during 1999 undertook survey and tissue sampling efforts at Tern Island to document and monitor PCB contamination in seals and reef fishes. Service funding was used by the Corps of Engineers to complete sea wall reconstruction design. These shore protection measures are intended to reduce erosion and minimize entrapment of seals.

At Tern Island, NMFS personnel carefully monitor the health and state of the population during pupping season. Weaned pups are tagged and measured. Yearlings are measured for a number of health factors. During 2000, NWR staff continued to assist in a shark study at French Frigate Shoals. The researchers observed interactions between large [primarily Galapagos and tiger] sharks and seals to determine if sharks were a significant source of seal pup mortality in near-shore waters. The researchers also worked to determine frequency of visits of individual sharks to the waters of the atoll using radio tracking devices. FWS personnel collect marine debris and flotsam from the beaches of Tern Island on a biweekly basis to prevent entanglement hazards. Tern Island FWS staff also assisted NMFS staff in a large marine debris survey and cleanup effort conducted in the waters of the atoll in August 2000. A daily patrol of the seawall was conducted to detect any seals that may have been washed over the deteriorating seawall and become trapped. Any seals found were relocated to the nearest beach. Efforts by the Service and the Corps of Engineers to finalize plans for replacement and repair of portions of the seawall continued in year 2000. The repairs will reduce erosion and minimize entrapment hazards for the monk seal. Finally, as part of the Hawaiian Monk Seal Recovery Project, marine fauna was collected from the Refuge for nutritional value analysis and fatty acid signatures for monk seal diet studies.

During 2000 at Laysan Island, Service personnel assisted in bleaching numbers on pups weaned late in the season, re-sighted tagged seals, and reported seal entanglements in marine debris. Service personnel also assisted in untangling seals from marine debris and collected marine debris from beaches regularly to reduce hazards. In February 2000, there was an alarming occurrence of aborted monk seal fetuses at Laysan. This event precipitated an unscheduled visit by NMFS personnel to Laysan Island. The Service offered assistance in terms of housing and cooking facilities, communications, and availability of Service personnel to assist when needed.

Midway Atoll National Wildlife Refuge Activities-Hawaiian Monk Seal
The Midway Atoll Hawaiian monk seal (Monachus schauinslandi) population remains at between 50-60 animals. A total of 12 pups were born in 1999, one more than in 1998. Monk seal-related activities at Midway were conducted under NMFS Permit No. 1-29 and Fish and Wildlife Special Use Permit MID-03-99. In 1999, personnel from the Refuge, NMFS, Hawaii Wildlife Fund, and Oceanic Society assisted in the recovery of the Hawaiian monk seal population at Midway by: (1) monitoring population numbers; (2) identifying, tagging, and bleach marking seals; (3) recording beach use patterns; (4) photo documenting seal behavior; and (5) determining prey preference by collecting and analyzing scats and spewings.

Service personnel embarked on an aggressive effort to document, map, and remove entangling net debris from Midway's reefs. A total of approximately 29,000 pounds of debris was removed during 1999.

Also in 1999, Service personnel assisted in the collection of reef fish and other marine species in support of monk seal diet studies. In addition, reef transects were initiated in selected areas to document abundance of monk seal prey species (lobster, octopus, eels, etc.). Service personnel also assisted NMFS personnel and other cooperators in

health assessment activities at Midway, involving collection of fat, blood, and fecal samples, as well as bacterial swabs, from several seals. Service personnel participated in extensive observations of, and interaction with, refuge visitors to monitor compliance with in-place refuge regulations to minimize disturbance of monk seals and other wildlife. This also included presentation of monk seal lectures and other interpretive tours, maintenance of trails, placement of informational signs, and development of observation sites.

Midway Atoll NWR staff remained active in protecting the Hawaiian Monk seal during 2000. Service volunteers, interested Refuge visitors, and staff and volunteers of nonprofit organizations joined the Refuge staff to recover entangling debris within the lagoon, emergent reef, and island beaches of the atoll. The Refuge collected about 27,000 pounds of debris between January and December.

The activities described here are funded through the normal Refuge operations budget. No specific funding from other sources is received. One Refuge staff member serves on the Hawaiian monk seal recovery team.

Midway Atoll National Wildlife Refuge Activities-Spinner Dolphin
The following activities were conducted on spinner dolphin (Stenella longirostris) under NMFS General Authorization No. 31 and Fish and Wildlife Special Use Permit MID-07-99.

In 1999, personnel from the Refuge, Oceanic Society, and Texas A&M University conducted the third year of a research project designed to assess impacts of human activities on Midway's

spinner dolphins. The objectives of the study are to: (1) assess abundance and distribution; (2) determine patterns of habitat use; (3) determine size, composition, and social structure of dolphin groups; (4) develop a photo identification file for the population; (5) document year-round activity pattern; and (6) evaluate dolphin behavior to detect possible human/dolphin conflicts and make management recommendations to minimize human impacts.

Field studies in 1999, in photo identification of known animals, led to a revised atoll population estimate of about 250 animals. In-water observation and photography in 1999, coupled with above water observations, significantly expanded information on the demographic structure and social behavior of the Midway dolphin school.

The activities described here are funded through the normal refuge operations. No specific funding from other sources is received.

USFWS

Hawaiian monk seal